the mom Babes

A Motherhood Anthology. ♥ Volume 2

CHRISTINA WALSH
CAROLYN TURKINGTON

TSPA The Self Publishing Agency, Inc.

Christina Walsh, Carolyn Turkington

The MomBabes: A Motherhood Anthology. Volume 2

TSPA The Self Publishing Agency, Inc.

First Edition

Softcover ISBN: 978-1-7776014-3-0
eBook ISBN: 978-1-7776014-4-7

Editor | Tara McGuire
Cover & Book Design | Kristy Twellmann Hill
Publishing Support | TSPA The Self Publishing Agency, Inc.

♥

To the MomBabe community

What began as an experiment in community has quite literally become a community. It is motherhood; it is womanhood; it is...*our* sisterhood.

Table of Contents

Foreword

Welcome back!

At the beginning of 2020, we had one year of 'being' MomBabes under our belts. We felt the excitement of a new decade looming and all of our business goals and dreams spooled out before us. We were all about reminding moms to put themselves at the top of the list. We issued a big fat permission slip for some self-love and showing up as our best selves.

Womp, womp. Ahem.

And then we had to pull a Ross Geller and pivot, PIVOT... PIVVVOTTT!!

We always talked about how one day we would write a book, but the concept seemed so far off in the future. One big reason was that we hadn't really figured out how. How would we actually do this? The universe delivered an opportunity and we decided to jump. Covid-19 fast-forwarded our dreams and we weren't going to wait. And good thing we didn't because...well, we're still living through that same pandemic.

The MomBabes: A Motherhood Anthology, twenty essays by twenty fine women, was published in May of 2021 and has been a huge success—both critically and emotionally. We are delighted and grateful. So, here we are doing it again.

We believe every woman can see a little bit of themselves in these stories. The pages are not full of suggestions, Top 10 lists to follow, or how to's, because we're not experts. Rather, these personal essays are the most meaningful pieces of our lives. Instead of offering advice, we offer you ourselves. Our hearts, our truths, our embarrassing confessions, biggest fears, and those little aha moments that keep us up at night. The women in this collection share their self-acceptance, and we want to offer the same grace to you.

We know now, we're here to help you write your life; to document a piece of your legacy. Just like us, we know that you have shifted, grown, and been tested this past year; perhaps you're still waiting to find the place where you feel fully seen and heard. Our hope is that you feel that *here*, in the *The MomBabes: A Motherhood Anthology Volume* 2.

The MomBabes Anthology is a collective memoir, written by women like you, for women like you. Welcome to a community with no membership required and no hidden fees. You belong here. We see you, we hear you, and heaven knows we *feel* you!

So, here we go! Eighteen incredible stories written by mothers who wanted to share a small but ever-so-valuable piece of themselves. We invite you to dive in, discover our shared experiences, and savour our mutual humanity.

We hope that you share the stories with your closest MomBabes and think about how you, too, have stories to share.

With much love and an extra shot of caffeine,

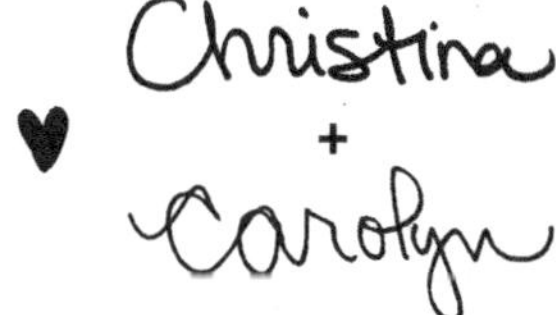

Nikki

♥

Sand Dollars

I remember when I decided "I was ready" to have kids, but it would be another three years before serendipity and science brought us our son.

My husband Marc and I were on a road trip in Washington state five years ago. We explored the Olympic Peninsula enroute to La Push, a small coastal community inside the Quileute Indian Reservation, to camp and surf. We nestled our tent in a little treed corner site, with a view of the ocean. With the beach just steps away, our surfboards and dog in tow, we were excited for a week of surf-camping.

My brother and I grew up in Quebec, but our great-uncle had a house on the beach in Maine and my mum took us there every summer. We'd all hop into Mum's old Buick Century with wood panelling, and drive about four and a half hours south east to spend a week or two. I remember winding down the window and smelling the pine trees mixed with the fresh salty air—a smell I would constantly be in search of for the rest of my life.

Those summer holidays taught me a lot about the power of the ocean—the waves and tides, carving out a permanent place in my heart. Twenty years later, I made my way to live on the West Coast so I could be by the mountains and ocean. When I follow my "blue heart," it only takes me to magical places.

So I suppose it is fitting that when I first decided it was time to have children I was on a beach, sand between my toes and the sound of waves echoing in my ears.

♥

We stayed in La Push for a couple of nights, got plenty of sand in our tent, attempted to paddle surf, drank cocktails on driftwood logs, and then headed to our next stop.

Neah Bay is the most northwesterly point in the continental United States—the beach itself is a beautiful horseshoe shape next to an open field campsite run by the Indigenous community. It's totally wild—no designated campsites, just $20 a night to stay.

We pitched our tent just steps from the beach trail in a private little nook, trees mostly surrounding us, and the sound of waves just beyond. We camped, cooked, played with our dog, and "surfed" the tiny little waves that rolled in.

One night after a few drinks, we walked out on the beach as dusk was creeping in. I found two sand dollars close enough together that I picked them both up.

With sand dollars in my hands and booze in my veins, I said to Marc, "I think I'm ready. I want to share moments like this with other little beings."

But it would be another few years of ups and downs, of ebbs and floods, until we successfully got pregnant. This story is about what happened in those years.

I'd hear the classic commentary, "It's not going to happen if you're stressed about it." So I silently declared, casting out my feelings to the universe as if to protect myself, "We are officially trying not to try!" That strategy didn't work so well. Our family doctor said that if we hadn't managed to naturally conceive in six months we should seek assistance.

I was self-employed as a personal trainer with clients in the studio and classes at different locations in town. Running around working split shifts, I began to feel like my fitness career was not conducive to my reproductive goals. In retrospect, my system was probably more often in "fight or flight mode" than not.

I consulted a naturopath who ran a bunch of blood tests, and we discovered that my progesterone levels were incredibly low. (Progesterone is the hormone that thickens the uterine lining, allowing the embryo to firmly implant itself in the uterus). She recommended natural fertility formulas during different parts of my cycle. An acupuncturist had me tracking my basal body temperature everyday, so I could learn when my hormones "surged" during ovulation.

This went on for a while until my gynecologist referred us and ran the gamut of standard infertility tests: blood work, pelvic ultrasounds, an HSG test, and hysteroscopies. I remember the antiseptic, sterile feeling of those medical clinics. Lying on my back during the HSG test, legs splayed waiting to be injected with dye by an older, white, bored, male doctor, blinded by the bright lights. The room was cold, and so was he. It felt like a voluntary assault on my femininity, for something I hadn't done.

The hysteroscopies felt like watching a live-version of the Discovery Channel, featuring myself. A doctor very gently, but indifferently inserting a wand up into my cervix to have a poke around. All I could do was breathe deeply to try and stay calm. I watched my insides live on-screen through the mechanical medical device inside my pelvis, while trying to relax to mitigate any cramping.

The doctor discovered uterine polyps. I was relieved. Removing a polyp could sometimes increase the chances of a positive pregnancy. I booked in for the routine half-day surgery, it's not major, but does require general anesthetic and a day of rest afterward.

After the removal, we met with the doctor at a fertility clinic, and decided that because a polyp removal can sometimes increase the chances of pregnancy, we would keep trying naturally for the time being.

Feelings of frustration, shame and inadequacy came flooding in like a king tide after every negative pregnancy test. When people I knew made pregnancy announcements, I felt envious.

Meanwhile, I was teaching Mom & Baby Fitness classes, watching other moms with their little ones, and training postpartum moms in the gym. I was happy to serve them, but I started to feel like I wasn't in personal alignment when I hadn't had a baby myself. Call it fitness imposter syndrome.

In early summer of 2018, a bout of severe pelvic pain signalled another polyp had grown back. Time was ticking.

After the second polyp was removed we decided it was time to move fast before another one grew back. I booked in with

Olive Fertility and in January we started the first round of fertility drugs.

I made some lifestyle changes: eased off the heavy drinking, cut way back on endurance cardio, and lifted lighter weights, I stopped intermittent fasting and obsessing about food choices, which was liberating. Under my naturopath's care I eliminated alcohol, caffeine, processed carbs and sugars. I got acupuncture regularly. And I read a book called *Making Babies* which helped me understand the current state of my body and its hormones. I also decided to take a break from my fitness career—the running around was keeping my nervous system in a sympathetic state, not conducive to making babies.

The fertility clinic started me on Clomid, a standard fertility drug, and every morning I drove in the grey, wet traffic of a Vancouver winter to have my blood tracked. When a surge was detected, they gave me a trigger shot to jump-start ovulation, and we were sent home to get it done.

After the first round failed, feelings of inadequacy flooded back in. I rode out the tsunami of shame and had to build myself back up again to face another attempt.

The next month, in early February, we travelled to see our families in Quebec. Marc and I were lying in bed early one morning when the phone rang. Marc's uncle/godfather had just passed away overnight. Uncle John had been married, but had never had children.

We returned to BC, and our next "attempt" at the clinic landed on Family Day. We did IUI (Intrauterine Insemination) this time—"the turkey baster" method. Just before I was inseminated, I asked the nurse if she was absolutely 100% certain the sperm belonged to my husband. Had she never seen *Jane the Virgin*?!

On March 7, the phone rang and it was a nurse calling from Olive. "You might want to sit down for this," she paused. "You're pregnant."

I was in complete shock. "Shut up!"

I will never forget the joy of that moment, my complete sense of disbelief after so much mystery. I cried tears of relief and joy.

I arrived home to a beautiful bouquet of flowers—the perfect culmination of a three-year journey of high hopes and low letdowns. I thought back to those sand dollars from three years before. The universe had delivered, and there was no sliver of a doubt in my mind that Marc's uncle John had something to do with it. Call it the circle of life, angels, reincarnation, whatever you want, but I know that the timing was significant and he somehow played a part.

Even though our journey was long and trying, I still felt some sense of guilt about getting pregnant after only one try with IUI. I know so many other women who have faced harder paths with miscarriages and multiple rounds of IVF, etc... almost as though my hardship wasn't hard enough.

I had a condition called "circumvallate placenta"—a structural weakness in the placenta that caused some intra-uterine growth restriction and premature labour—it was terrifying.

Jake was born September 25, 2019, at thirty-three weeks and five days gestational age. He was tiny, but mighty, weighing in at just four pounds.

We stayed with Jake in the NICU for three weeks while he grew and learned to feed without the gastric-nasal tube. I was in and out of the NICU three times per day for visits and feedings. Once he was a little stronger, we started breastfeeding for a bit, then topping him up with the tube. I would breastfeed, put him back in his incubator, then go pump for another ten to fifteen minutes. I nicknamed myself Betsy.

Finally, on Thanksgiving weekend, we took Jake home. I remember feeling terrified of leaving the hospital and our "professional babysitters" to bring home a barely five-pound infant. We were coming home with our newborn, and also to nest in our new home. We had just taken possession of a cozy log house on a road with no lines painted down the middle. It reminded me of the log home I grew up in, built by my dad.

For years I had dreamed of a baby, and of moving north up the Sea-to-Sky to a full-time home, and in one giant, peeling tidal wave, the stork, the lab techs, and the realtor delivered.

♥

As I write this, Thanksgiving 2021 just passed, marking exactly two years since we first brought Jake home from the hospital. And exactly one month ago, we found out we are pregnant with our second child, naturally. I was in disbelief again—but this time because it happened without the help of a fertility clinic. We are so grateful (and scared!) to bring another little boy into our family.

I think back to that night at Neah Bay, when I picked up those two sand dollars, somehow knowing they represented our two future children. I see them every day on the windowsill in our bedroom, and know there is something serendipitous in them.

♥

If you want a full day of multi-sport activities planned, including headstands on paddleboards, ask Nikki. Weekends find her running through the Squamish rainforest followed by a cold dip in the creek. She combines her passion for movement with her career helping women move and train for birth, and ease back to their favourite activities postpartum. If you want to make her really happy, take Nikki away anywhere hot, Spanish, with a surf break.

@SEATOSKYFITNESS

Longing for Belonging

My mom was ten years old when she left India to come to Canada. With many hopes, dreams, and aspirations, the family moved to Squamish, BC. Back in the early 1960s, her family was one of the first three Indo-Canadian families to settle there. While my grandfather was busy working full-time at the lumber mill, my grandmother was equally busy raising her children and trying to fit into her new setting. I can only imagine how hard this was for my grandparents, it was the colliding of two cultures.

Coming from a culture that was much more strict, my mom and her siblings were limited in what they could participate in. My grandmother upheld Indian traditions expected from a wife such as cooking, cleaning and taking care of the children, and in turn she expected her children to follow traditions as well. Consequently, my mom was not able to do things like wear shorts or makeup and there would be no sleepovers with friends or dating. There were several times in her younger years when she felt frustrated with her parents as she struggled to gain independence, freedom, and growth. While most of her friends were out with boys, and attending school dances, she was at home helping out with chores and taking care of her younger siblings. Her parents were new to this country and they were willing to adapt and change, but this would not happen overnight.

When my mom came to Canada at ten years old she was placed in Grade 1 due to her limited English skills. At the end of Grade 10, when most of her classmates were fifteen, she was eighteen and was taken back to India for an arranged marriage. I can see how she would have wondered if she was moving forward or in fact taking a step backwards. My mom told me about her first encounter with my dad. In India, the man is shown different pictures of women to essentially select a wife from. When she met my dad for the first time, they were given a few minutes to speak in private. He told her that if she was feeling doubtful and was uncomfortable he would tell his family that she wasn't right for him. You see, traditionally men could say no and reject the woman, but it was not acceptable for the women to do so. This thoughtful gesture made her feel as though he considered her feelings. She saw his kindness which brought her some ease in an otherwise confusing situation. Wise technique on his part—well played Dad! After they married, she applied for him to come to Canada and in the years that followed his family would also immigrate here.

Because of her experiences and struggles, my mom was determined that her own children would fit in more easily. My parents had four daughters. As the eldest, it was my job to pave the way for my sisters. My mom's passion for allowing us the freedom she longed for was often challenged by my father. After all, he was newer to this country and its ways. My dad had not experienced the same hardships she had. He was very set in his ways and believed in our culture's traditions much more than she. As we grew up and as she allowed us some freedom she quickly realized his views were much different on the matter. But she stayed true to her feelings and wishes to allow us the ability to fit in.

I have many fond memories of my school days, and I also remember the ways I felt isolated and out of place. You see, there were not a lot of brown kids in the '70s in the small town of Squamish. I felt the difference between me and my white friends. I wasn't exactly like them but I also wasn't exactly like the kids of my culture either. It was different for me because most of the brown kids were not permitted to join sports teams, have playdates, go to the school dance and so on. Thanks to my mom, I was allowed to join ballet, wear shorts in gym class, cut my hair, wear skirts and makeup, shave my legs, and eventually even have a boyfriend! Dating was 100% not allowed in our culture.

Although it was great to participate in all those activities, it caused problems too. The brown girls my age judged me—they were jealous because they were not allowed to do those things. It was odd getting those vibes and comments from them. I mean, wasn't I one of them? I wasn't white, but it seemed that I no longer fit in with the girls from my culture either. Being free also made me different; as though I didn't belong anywhere completely. So who could I identify with?

I felt a sort of reverse racism, if you will, which left me unsure and insecure. Had my culture turned on me?...or had I turned on my culture? Funny how as much as my mom tried to help me fit in I still didn't, in fact perhaps the opposite. Now, I was the one struggling to integrate with my own traditions and culture.

From a young age I would say "I am going to marry someone Italian not Indian." I was quite adamant about it.

My grandmother would hear me and say, "Shhhhhh, don't let people hear you say that. What will they think?" It was looked down upon to marry out of the culture.

True to my words, in Grade 9 I met my Italian. I was fifteen and he was four years my senior. We got married when I was twenty-one. My mother's side of the family accepted it fairly well but my father's side was much more traditional and didn't come around as easily.

My marriage was only the second interracial marriage on my dad's side of the family. My older cousin was first. There had been a lot of resistance when she announced she was getting married to someone white and now I was experiencing that tension. Once again, I questioned where I belonged, torn between two worlds and two cultures. As a result, we had two weddings. One in a church, where I wore a beautiful white wedding gown and veil, and the very next day an Indian wedding ceremony in our local Sikh Temple, wearing a traditional red Indian outfit.

Heart Explosion! When I had my first child, I finally knew I belonged to something 100% for the first time in my life. I worried less about my cultural struggle. In fact, motherhood had a way of consuming me completely. I had no idea I could love so much. Motherhood brought me so much joy and still does to this day. But then, as my kids grew up and needed me less, the question of where I fit in slowly returned.

No one wants their marriage to fail. No one wants to break their family unit. Eleven years into our marriage we got divorced. Failure, guilt, and even shame to name a few of the big feels. I could hear all the "I told you so's." Not from my immediate family, but I knew what most people from our culture were thinking...that they knew it wouldn't last, that I should have married someone within my culture, it would have been better and easier. I felt as though they thought that I had made a mistake. But it wasn't a mistake: my marriage brought me the two biggest joys of my life, my two beautiful children, the centre of my world.

I was determined to keep the children's best interests in mind at all times even though there were days when I woke up feeling lost, alone, and scared. I put all my effort into having a healthy relationship with their father and we had a very civil separation and divorce. We didn't fight over the children or over their custody. We put them front and centre and joined forces to ensure their every need was met. It wasn't easy, but it was very important to both of us.

At thirty-three, I wondered how anyone else could ever get to know me, I mean all of me. The thought of finding someone new was overwhelming, yet I knew that I didn't want to be alone. How would I trust again? The familiar feelings of loneliness, confusion, and not knowing where I belonged returned. I was too tired after all I had been through. Too tired to explain. Too tired to share. So that was that. Or so I thought.

This time I found someone within my culture. Problem solved right?...maybe not. In our culture divorce was frowned upon and second marriages were really frowned upon. You see, a woman that was previously married, had children, and divorced was considered used goods and it wasn't because my new husband made me feel this way. As much as I felt "Canadian," my own feelings and ingrained cultural judgements sabotaged me. If getting remarried was wrong or taboo, what was my other choice? I was lost and confused again.

After dating for over a year, I was able to let my guard down and to allow myself to feel love, acceptance and happiness. I was ready to embrace the future and we decided to get married. We created a blended family and I became a stepmom to three. My second marriage has brought me much happiness, we have been married for fourteen years now, we have accomplished a lot together, we continue to defy the odds, grow, learn and love.

Heartbreak. In 2016 I experienced grief like never before. I lost both my grandparents: first my grandmother, Nannie age 89 and then 40 days later my grandfather, Nanna age 92. My Nannie was my closest connection to my culture, who was I without her? I felt lost, uneasy and shaken. When Nanna passed the feeling was even more intense, as now it seemed my only real bloodline was gone too. I mean, I know I still had my parents and the rest of my family but I just couldn't help but feel like our entire family shook, as though we no longer had our foundation. The ties to my culture were gone, my security was gone, and I felt abandoned once again. It was like my family roots had disappeared.

As I look back over the years that have spread over two cultures I love; the joy of motherhood and devastation of divorce; the loss of my grandparents and the love in my second marriage have all shaped the woman I am today. Although some of my experiences have affected me in negative ways, I choose to focus on the positive impacts: I am resilient, patient, understanding, and I have the ability to adapt to life's ever-changing circumstances. To some, I may come across as thick-skinned but I can actually be quite sensitive. I am very guarded with my heart, and I don't let others get close to me easily. But those few that I do let in, I give myself to completely.

As I age and try to understand where I belong, I wonder if maybe I was never really lost at all? Perhaps I don't need to fit into one category. Perhaps this soul-searching journey of mine has led me right back to me. Maybe being me is enough and maybe I belong everywhere.

Ruby loves all things home-related: she's a great decorator and owns a new home construction and renovation company. Designing cabinetry is her favourite part! Ruby is obsessed with sourdough and makes a killer guacamole—it's possible she was Mexican in a former life. If you see her light on at night, that's just her overactive brain keeping her awake.

A COLLECTIVE STORY
WRITTEN BY THE BRACKENDALE BABES

Birds of a Feather

As soon as I answered the phone my heart stopped and my stomach curled into knots. The voice belonged to my dear friend, you know the one, the one that NEVER asks for anything and would give you her headlamp and safety vest on a dark wet walk through the neighborhood, yeah that one, she needed help.

The first thing out of her mouth was, "Jen's been taken to the hospital and Dan wants us to go tell the girls and stay with them until he gets home with an update."

With a polite but firm "HELL NO," I declined her offer, suggesting she find someone more suitable for the job. After all, I'm the event planner who pulls us together to celebrate our wins and toast each other with a glass of wine, and oftentimes the one that has no filter and is pulling my foot out of my mouth. I am definitely not the one that handles the hard, emotionally scary life-changing events. My lovely friend replied in her calm, kind way: "I will see you at Jen's house in five minutes." Sigh...

The evolution of the Brackendale Babes started long before that unforgettable day.

In 2009, I gathered with a group of moms in the library of our kids' school listening and learning about a new event coming to our sleepy small town of Squamish, BC—The Relay for Life. This 12-hour overnight walking relay had a festival atmosphere, bringing the community together to celebrate life and raise money to fight cancer. The slogan of the event was, "Cancer Doesn't Sleep and Neither Do We!" That resonated with us and gave us a reason to leave mom life behind and for twelve hours focus on our friendship and the contribution we were making to our community!

Having a common goal would bring together a very diverse group of women—including a nurse, a pharmacist, a massage therapist, and the owner of a local electrical company—and that diverse group would change each other's lives in ways we couldn't imagine. That initial twelve hours of walking, cheering, laughing and competing would eventually grow into an unbreakable bond of unity that continues today.

Our initial meeting at a local neighborhood restaurant brought together ten distinctly different women, with their own lives and challenges, all trying their best at this crazy roller coaster ride we call motherhood. Among the group were stay-at-home moms, working moms, shifting-worker moms, and single moms, all of which offered unique talents and something special to the group. The message was clear from our first gathering that our fundraising events and efforts were going to emphasize the FUN in fundraising.

We created many annual events, such as the Daddy/Daughter Dance—imagine a Disney setting with little princesses arriving with their fathers dressed up and dancing the night away—and the Tapas Bike Tour, which consisted of forty women on their cruiser bikes riding around town enjoying bubbly and bruschetta along the way, complete with pink boas blowing in the wind! There was also the annual garage sale that received the strangest items for donation, for instance, a life-size ceramic potbelly pig with a cigar hanging out of its mouth. We laughed as these obscure items were scooped up by some proud new owner to put on display on their front porch.

The individual strength of the women within the group empowered us as a whole. We each brought different skills to the table, sponsorship seekers, organizational queens, and roll-up-your-sleeves worker bees. This array of skill sets collectively got sh*t done, all while raising kids, working jobs, and running houses. The bonding that arose through the chaos of fundraising was much more valuable than any money raised. The Brackendale Babes became an impenetrable army of sisterhood.

A year into our fundraising shenanigans, we were gifted fifty pink plastic flamingos and the idea of "Flocking" was born. Imagine this...ten women dressed in black, waiting in the dark to place fifty flamingos on some unsuspecting person's yard! Just being out at night without our kids was exciting enough, but add in jumping through bushes and rolling in the ditch to avoid being detected, and we were hooked on this mom rush. The unsuspecting victim was then required to pay a lump sum amount to have the flamingos removed from their yard and placed in a new location. We lost count of how many flockings we pulled off but each one pushed our fundraising goal a little higher and we felt like we were telling cancer to "FLOCK OFF!". We adopted the flamingo as our mascot and became known for our spirit of adventure and the ever-present pink boa.

Eventually, The Relay for Life event ended in Squamish but we were not ready to have the FUN-raising shenanigans end, so our efforts were turned to community initiatives that needed support, including the Squamish Hospital, Howe Sound Women's Center and a few local families. The community enjoyed these events as much as we did and the impact of the Brackendale Babes was reaching further than even we realized. We sensed the anticipation and excitement building as local women would contact us in late spring every year eager to participate in the Tapas Bike Tour.

In addition to the FUN-raising events, we also took time to celebrate. There were birthdays, Christmas parties, and weekend getaways to name a few. One time, we rented a remote cabin in the woods to rest, rejuvenate, and celebrate with each other. Imagine a group of women, some fit, some not, some outgoing and some modest, but all accepted for who they are, frolicking in the forest with a glass of wine in hand, completely oblivious to potential onlookers as our faith in and support of each other flourished through naked vulnerability. The love and trust between us deepened in that moment of raw and exposed acceptance of one another.

We continued to keep the fun in fundraising for a few more years until burnout hit and life took over—parents dying, marriages breaking down, and feeling too stretched to continue. We were tired, so tired, but now what? What happens to the unity, solidarity, and community that has developed over the years? Would it be strong enough to sustain without a stated purpose or fundraising goals? What would connect us and keep us in touch with one another? With the "reason" shifting would the bond also shift? Would it disappear completely? We all felt the fear as we sat together laughing, crying, and toasting our glasses to the past, present, and hopefully the future of the Brackendale Babes.

The Brackendale Babes are always ready to roll up their sleeves to get sh*t done and eager to hop in the "vangina" (the family mini-van which got its name from being packed full of Babes during our road trips) for the next adventure! Our YOLO (you only live once) attitude can be felt when we are hiking the trails, enjoying a meal together or when we take off for the weekend as a group! Each time we are together our love and support for one another grows a little deeper and it feels like this is the glue that will hold us together for years to come.

We are all independent, capable women who have graciously learned to accept and appreciate help when needed, even if we didn't ask. We may not have been saplings in the forest together but the friendships that have developed over the past decade are like the rings inside a cedar tree: they have grown into a circle of friendship that stands the test of time and weathers life's storms together.

These resilient, caring, strong, vulnerable, funny, and unique women are able to get "raw" with one another, even feeling naked at times, standing side by side, arm in arm, ready to tackle what life throws at us next. The genuine, heartfelt, compassionate support is never-ending and will be the legacy that the Brackendale Babes pass on to other women. Encouraging them to raise their glasses and make sure they know they are FLOCKING FABULOUS!

As the Brackendale Babes mature, the rings of the cedar tree have thickened, integrated and expanded, and the support is far-reaching and unwavering. The sisterhood will continue, ensuring we are safely buckled in on the roller coaster of life and one day when we are old birds, we will live side by side with a flamingo perched on each of our lawns so we can find our way home from the pub.

That phone call long ago changed our lives forever and initially, we struggled to understand why this happened but we now realize we were being sent a message to surround our sister in love and to take care of even the smallest detail so she could recover fully. Since that phone call, our bond has strengthened and made us even more grateful for one another and we know that showing up in the same room makes us better humans. These ten women are connected in a special way that even we don't understand and have stopped trying to figure out. We know that the phone may ring again. However, we all sleep a little sounder knowing that the Brackemdale Babes sisterhood will have the courage to answer the call.

♥

The Brackendale Babes is a powerhouse collective of women from Brackendale, BC (duh!) who are really good at showing up, digging deep, and getting sh*t done. Antics may include dancing wildly to The Paperboys at the BAG, assembling Christmas baskets for youth in need, or sitting quietly holding space for one another and saying nothing. Whatever we are doing, there is always a YOLO undertone and a grateful feeling to be in the same room with these amazing, unique women.

@MCINTOSH.LISA

Arlene Kate Jen

Camille

Chantal

Felicia Julie

Lisa

Karen

here's your
PERMISSION SLIP:

to SAY NO
to START AGAIN
to GROW
to BE YOURSELF
to do NOTHING
to be IN LOVE *with* YOU

Lisa

♥

Becoming Me

Dear Mom and Dad,

So this is fifty. I say this with a flat tone. My voice is not an enthusiastic roar screaming "forty is the new fifty." Exclamation point. I do not feel Fab! I feel dull, upside down, shaken. I feel more than a bit lost and sad. It's been just over two months since Dad's passing, making it official that I am now parentless.

I am untethered and alone without the greatest influences and most supportive people in my life. Granted, I can find perspective: I'm not a child orphaned, nor am I a moody teenager in the crux of discovering herself while losing a parent. I'm a married (albeit unhappily), middle-aged adult with two teenage children, who has created a life of her own and can handle challenging emotional setbacks and failures, and survive. I am resilient. But I've lost my favourite people, my second self.

I miss you both with a deepness and longing that I could not have anticipated. I feel alone without my guideposts to run my questions past and reveal my insecurities and fears when I need a voice I can trust. Nothing very unique here, except I didn't see this coming, at least not your death, Dad, just four years after Mom. I am unhinged and emotionally depleted. I have never felt less like myself. I have never felt more grown-up than these past few months without you in my life, just a phone call or short commute away. Mom, I know this honesty share would make you in particular cringe. You'd react stiffly with an irritated and disappointed tone, "Oh Lisa." The same tone I heard all my life whenever I expressed bold, honest emotions that you preferred left hidden under the surface.

Truth is, I'm static in the significant areas of my life: marriage, career, and personal fulfilment. I have been complacent for a while. I know it, my friends know it. You both recognized it, but we didn't talk about it. I shared my frustrations, but you were protective and told me to take care of my family. "We want you to be happy," you stated all of my adult life. An easy phrase, but no explanation as to how. So, I kept trudging through, not wanting to disrupt my family. I chose convenience over fulfilment—my convenience, other people's convenience, at the cost of my own fulfilment.

When the kids were little, I did the full-out, exhausting, working-mom routine at a job I had a level of satisfaction with. I did the daycare routine, was the soccer coach, PAC volunteer, resident cook and activity scheduler. Until, after five demanding years, feeling unsupported, I couldn't do it anymore. I recognized I was unhappy and burnt out, so I jumped off this working-mom merry-go-round permanently to step back and reassess—and six weeks later, Mom, you died.

During those early years when the kids were so young, you both told me to slow down and enjoy these moments. But I was always on the go, dropping by to see you with the kids for a quick visit or meal, then off to somewhere or other. I was caught up in that repeat cycle of getting through life versus truly enjoying it. Yes, there was much joy and many first milestones sandwiched between the years, and so much time that R and C got to spend with you both, but I knew in my heart that life could look and feel differently—truer to me and more satisfying.

Being married with children was your big wish for me. I felt this and heard this a lot growing up in our traditional household. When I made the decision to leave my job to devote more time to caring for you, Mom, the universe shifted and time seemed to speed up. I had hoped to make up for all the shitty adolescent years of angry, disrespectful behaviour I directed towards you, but that didn't happen. Within two weeks of that new year, you entered the hospital...and never came out.

You died, and I became a motherless daughter at forty-six. And my first, very deep experience with grief began—that yearning for more time and many thoughts of regret, couched between helping R and C process their very first significant family loss, planning a funeral, acting as spokesperson for our wide network of family and friends, while supporting Dad in his shock, grief, and loneliness.

After almost two years of moving forwards in life without you, Mom, it was your turn, Dad, to experience two major surgeries without a devoted partner by your side. Your strong recovery was followed by a crazy year of the COVID-19 pandemic. And then 2021 began with a shocking new health finding. Within seven months of diagnosis, and a cancer journey that was relentless, swift, painful, and crippling, you were gone too, Dad.

Caring for you at home for the last three months of your life was the greatest privilege and honour of my life. With the heartbreaking and often unbearable pain of losing you both, I feel like I have finally stepped into the revered title of 'adult,' yet I still feel very much a confused child. Shit suddenly got real and hard. Life is less secure. I don't have you to fall back on, to catch my fall. You are no longer here to help guide me, regardless of the fact that I am a grown-up responsible for teenagers of my own.

Mom and Dad, two months since Dad's passing and my current state is...lacklustre. With your passing Mom, I was in action putting everyone else's needs over mine, but with Dad's passing, I find myself falling apart in a way I never did with my grief for you. I stay up far too late, too often. I don't get enough sleep. I yell too much. I'm reactive. I am short-tempered with the kids, D, myself, and the silly inconsequential things that come up, like messes left on the counter or tripping over the kids' crap left in the hallway. I scream *fuck!* a lot. I enjoy my comfortable loungewear far too much. I misplace, lose, and forget things these days: keys, jackets, my phone, and recently my return flight home from visiting my girlfriends in Terrace. I showed up one hour after the flight had departed. I relied on my memory!? These days? I deliver the kids to appointments on the wrong days. Almost daily I scroll photos/videos of you both on my phone and cry. These are my diminishing coping skills. This is grief. I recognize that.

I read countless articles about grief and follow grief accounts on Instagram. Talking to my girlfriends brings comfort. This current dedicated focus on writing is a positive, satisfying thing that I am doing for myself to move forwards with intention and create some joy.

I want to be a morning person, or at least I like the idea of it. I am a perennial night owl—thanks to you, Mom. I am productive late at night. It's quiet, I'm alone and finally no one needs anything from me. But lately, I watch The National and then instead of retiring to bed, I'll scroll Facebook or watch the

Kardashians. Who am I? I rationalize it's to turn my brain off and enjoy some solitude. But I know it's procrastination and avoidance. And grief.

I've let my discipline and my fitness go. I've gained some weight. I'm not eating enough vegetables. I bake every kind of recipe with pumpkin: pumpkin bread, muffins, bars. All the carbs! I eat standing at the counter. Most of the time I don't take much care with my appearance. Don't get me wrong...I shower daily and wear deodorant, but I don't make a lot of effort—leggings and running shoes are sooo comfortable. I relish the predictability of my daily uniform that is not polished nor shows any effort created with a confining zipper, buttons or collars.

Mom and Dad, over the years you reminded me to slow down and not take on everything. Volunteering fuels me and it feels good to be of service—traits I learned from you both. But now I see that my service work prevents me from looking at myself and my needs. I hide behind this cloak of "service." I write down goals, then move on with no intention of fulfilling them. I want to actually achieve my personal goals. I want to live with more joy. I need to challenge myself beyond the mediocre. Like Cher yelled at hapless Nicolas Cage in the movie *Moonstruck*, with a forcible slap to the face, I need to "Snap out of it!"

My entire life I have worn the crown of "good daughter" because showing up for you was very important to me. You meant everything to me, even when my selfish actions and mean words suggested otherwise. At times I was conflicted with the demands I placed on this role, while balancing the new roles of wife and mother and trying to please everyone. As I grew older, I became aware of your mortality and always wanted to put your needs first. For too long I took your love for granted because you were always there for me. Always. In declining health, your comfort was paramount to me and I was at your service when needed, especially to you, Dad, after Mom's passing. The sacrifices you both made for your three kids was never lost on me. You raised us with unconditional love, kindness, and security. This notion of security granted me a sense of comfort but also pushed me to take the safe route at times, unfortunately.

With your deaths, an important part of my sense of security or identity has been shaken. I feel a shift taking place in my life and it's time to step over many personal constructs that are holding me back from happiness and my best self. The people I loved the most and wanted to please the most are gone. I can now fail miserably while trying, without the fear of upsetting you, or causing you worry. Mom and Dad, I am at a crossroads and I have been heading this way for the last few years. Soon I'll be fifty-one. A lifetime of your loving armour that enveloped me like a warm hug has been released. Moving forwards, slowly, I am certain of my next actions. It's time to start making some hard decisions about my life, my relationship, about what makes me thrive.

Mom and Dad, you were my anchors who kept me steady and in place, particularly when I became a wife and parent and entered the rocky seas of parent life. You were my safe harbour to vent and gain support. Without you both as my anchor, I can change direction and course—changes that may not be traditional or comfortable in your eyes and will cause discomfort and hardships that you tried to protect me from. But I have gained a clear understanding that my freedom and growth are worth the discomfort. I no longer have to act in a way that pleases you. I can act for myself without fear of disapproval.

As I pack up your home and your life, I feel overwhelming grief. But I have also found clarity, strength, and a path forward. Your premature deaths have impacted the urgency of the rest of my life. If I am lucky to surpass the age of eighty, that means I will be blessed with thirty more years of living. Playing it safe has robbed me, to a degree, of my passion and possibility. Security can be overrated and soul-draining. It's time to think big, deal with the setbacks, and start fresh.

I've never felt more dialled-in and focused on my needs and wants than right now. Your absence in my life has strengthened my resolve to move forward in action. I am finally ready to become me.

♥

Lisa asks a LOT of questions: her friends say she'd be a natural radio host. Her loud voice (and a fairly consistent stream of swear words) can be heard from across the soccer field whether she's playing or coaching her kids. Girlfriend chats over a glass of crisp white wine keep Lisa sane (and grounded) while her night owl tendencies and rainy Sunday morning soccer commitments keep her sleep-deprived.

Jen

Everything Isn't Fine

You were barely pregnant anyways.

After five years of marriage, my husband Colin and I had stopped 'taking precautions,' but we weren't actively trying. We were seeing what would happen. Just before Christmas, I took a home pregnancy test and was surprised to see two pink lines appear. I went to the doctor to confirm and that test came back negative. Hmmm...what was going on? I was sent for blood work. Those results came back positive.

A few weeks into the new year, I went to the hospital because while I thought I was fine, I had started spotting. After waiting into the wee hours of the morning, a doctor slid the curtain and entered the makeshift room. He flipped a page, and without looking at me told me I was barely pregnant anyways.

Barely pregnant.

There was no conversation about how I might feel. There was no discussion that this may have been a shock or mention of how I should care for myself. Nothing. Just, come back in a few days for an ultrasound to ensure that it passed naturally.

It.

I was barely pregnant anyways.

Colin and I had only told one person about our pregnancy: my mom. Nobody else knew. I just carried on as if nothing had happened. As I was barely pregnant anyways, I didn't take time to care for myself or allow myself to go through grief. I was back at the office within five hours of finding out that at about seven weeks in my pregnancy, I had lost the baby. I told myself it would just be easier to go to work so I wouldn't have to reschedule meetings, or negotiate new timelines.

I wish I had taken time to care for myself. To cry, to curl up in bed, and to come to terms with the fact that I would never meet the baby Colin and I had created. I wish I had prioritized myself and what I needed.

Everything wasn't fine. The miscarriage set my baby-making clock into overdrive. For the next few months, Colin and I got busy. Very busy. We tracked my cycle, monitored my ovulation, scheduled an appointment with a specialist, and tried fertility acupuncture. Each month that passed had me questioning what was wrong with me. I still hadn't told many people that we'd had a miscarriage or that we were trying. I didn't want to talk about it. It was just too hard and uncomfortable. Besides, everything was fine.

Eight months after losing our first baby, we were pregnant again. Roughly nine months later, Dublin was born. She came almost two weeks early. I still was planning to work for a couple of more days when my water broke. For the first few hours of labour, before my contractions became hellish, I was on my laptop trying to wrap up commitments. Thirty-three hours later, we finally met her.

While I was overjoyed to be a mom, there were aspects of motherhood that were more challenging than I anticipated. Who knew I would bawl my eyes out reading Baby Beluga? Who knew I would miss working so much? How much I craved using my brain? That I would struggle with the inertia of mommy and baby activities? Did I tell anyone this? No, of course not, because everything was fine.

Some of my friends were on maternity leave at the same time. We would take walks together, go for coffee (or in my case tea), dance around in stroller Zumba, stretch at mommy and baby yoga classes, and gather to discuss all things babies.

After one of those Zumba classes Dublin had a five-alarm poopout. Poop was all over Dublin, up her back, through her clothes and all over me, including my light pink workout shorts. It looked like I was the one who'd had an accident. I made a mad dash to buy new shorts. All I could do was laugh. What else are you going to do?

While I enjoyed seeing my friends and being a new mom, I missed the sense of accomplishment I received from working. I missed making decisions, feeling like I was providing value, talking and strategizing on how to solve complex issues. I missed receiving a paycheque, and I missed the freedom to get up and go whenever I wanted. How easy it used to be to run out for a quick errand.

I was in tears telling Colin I couldn't keep faking these mommy and baby get-togethers. I missed using other parts of my brain and I needed to go back to work.

When Dublin was around six months old, Colin took six weeks of parental leave and I went back to work as a Labour Relations Manager. Part of my professional development included negotiating a collective agreement. It was refreshing to make strategic decisions and to feel like I was making a difference. I wasn't just a mom anymore.

It was also hard. I was breastfeeding and needed to pump at work. My work area wasn't set up to pump and I didn't want to push the issue. I didn't want to ask for more. I already felt like it was an ask to come back to work. I wanted to feel and be seen as my old self, not just a mom. As a human resources professional, I ensured our organization did the right things for our employees, yet I struggled and felt vulnerable trying to advocate for myself. It was so much easier to support others.

Dublin wasn't sleeping through the night. In fact she wouldn't sleep through the night until she was almost five. Between working, pumping, and not sleeping I'm not sure how I got through it. That's what being a working mom is, right? Everything is fine.

Despite the exhaustion, I wanted another baby.

Shortly after Dublin turned one, we became pregnant again. In my first trimester, my brother Matthew passed away. He decided he no longer wanted to wait for a heart transplant; that he would rather refuse treatment than live the life he was living. He was only thirty, and had a very young daughter.

After a couple of days, I returned to work. Because everything was fine.

Shortly after that, I was on a work trip in Alberta when Colin called me. There was an emergency at Dublin's daycare. Dublin was safe, but I felt guilty for not being home to help navigate the emergency. I felt that I wasn't being a good parent to Dublin, or a good partner to Colin.

The daycare was shut down while the provider was investigated for leaving children, aged five and younger, alone while she took older children to school. That those younger children (Dublin included) were locked in a house with nobody there to watch them terrified me. Had Dublin been calling for help with nobody answering her? What if there had been a fire? What if she choked on something? What if, what if?

We pulled Dublin from her care. I can now see how the shock of her being in danger, and losing my brother, impacted my mental wellbeing during my pregnancy with Delaney.

Once again, I carried on working and pretended everything was fine. Work was stressful with the contentious but successful negotiation of a new collective agreement.

My pregnancy continued and I was tired, stressed, and putting on too much weight. Each day was a battle to get through. At eight months pregnant, I went on medical leave until Delaney was born.

The second time around, we were more prepared for what maternity and parental leave would look like for us. When Delaney was three months old, Colin took parental leave and we spent three months together as a family of four. Parks in the morning and parks in the afternoon. We visited friends in Edmonton, we travelled to Mexico. We bonded.

Colin and I went back to work when Delaney was six months old. Both kids entered daycare. I was still exhausted and found the commute challenging. Every day the same grind. Up at 5:30 a.m. Defrosting breast milk, breakfast, makeup, lunches, business clothes. Leave the house by 6:40 a.m. Drop the kids at daycare. Race to the SkyTrain station. Walk the last six blocks to the Vancouver office. Work like crazy. Pump in the bathrooms. Try to climb that corporate ladder. Apply for promotions and be declined. Race to get the kids. Or go straight home to try to feed them by 6 p.m. Cleanup time. Story time. Bedtime. Jump on my laptop to try to catch up on work. Dishes, laundry, kiss Colin on the cheek, collapse.

I didn't want to admit I was exhausted and overwhelmed. This was life with two career-driven parents. Everything was fine.

Shortly after returning to work, Colin and I both attended the We for She Conference in Vancouver. Colin stood up and spoke about taking parental leave. I was pumping in the bathroom. I caught the last bit and of course was proud of him for encouraging organizations to support fathers taking parental leave.

The kicker for me was how much he was celebrated for paving the way for other dads while I was being questioned for returning to work "early." Colleagues, family, and friends asked why I would go back after only six months. Did I have postpartum depression? No, I just needed more. It was okay for Colin to need more than just being a worker, but it wasn't okay for me to want more than just being a mom.

I wanted motherhood *and* a career.

Then the pandemic hit. My father's health was declining as he was in liver failure. He was extremely fortunate to receive a liver transplant and I became one of his primary caregivers during a tortuous three-month recovery. I saw a loved one relapse and then recover through their addiction. My grandma's health deteriorated and my father-in-law went through heart surgery. Life was tough and I questioned my mortality and how quickly things can change.

Through all of this, I continued to work full-time and hold it together for my husband and children, for my teams at work, for my friends and for my family. As I started to crumble under the immense pressure, I realized I couldn't keep pretending anymore.

Everything was not fine.

I needed my husband to hold me and remind me that we would get through this together. I needed my friends and family to talk to, and I needed to admit that I was having a hard time. I started counselling and continued my development by becoming a coach.

Through this education I began to understand the three spheres of control. What is within my control, what I can influence, and what is outside of my control. By realizing what I needed to let go, I was able to release so much pressure.

It was also through loved ones holding space for me, journalling, and personal growth that I realized it's okay not to be fine every day. That while being a mom is rewarding and challenging, it isn't the only thing that defines who I am. I started to set boundaries and prioritize myself and what I needed. I learned the power of saying no. So freeing to let go of expectations.

And today, I take life as it comes and everything really, truly, is fine.

Jennifer cannot live without her husband and kids, tea, a good book, and ChapStick! Thinking about work and the endless things that need to happen can keep her up at night. She is a super-fast reader and makes the best chocolate chip cookies. She once dreamed of owning a bookstore where shoppers could drink wine and tea (it's not too late, Jennifer!) She's such a great singer that her husband banned her from the family karaoke machine.

Lana

Exactly The Same, But Totally Different

"*I'm getting married in a castle in England!*"

"*The fuck you are*," said Coronavirus, sounding suspiciously like Jason Bateman.

'Rona, the new kid in town. What a little puke. I hoped scientists would kick the crap out of him behind the arena after school.

In the blissfully unsuspecting early months of 2020, I was engaged to a "Fritish" man who let me have the pickle off every one of his burgers and loved my toothless, sometimes wheelchair-bound, pug. Okay fine, I often make up words. He is both French and British, you know, Fritish. We had just paid a significant deposit on our dream wedding in a castle that was smaller than Downton Abbey but bigger than my elementary school, with forty-one bedrooms and hopefully a couple of ghosts. We were moments from departure to the South of France to snuggle the newest baby to join the Fritish family. For real. This was my life and you are gawd damn right I was jazzed about it.

My life wasn't always this fairytale-sounding but it was turning out pretty darn fantastic. Then somewhere in the world a wombat farted on a carrot that was eaten by a human and BAM! We had a global pandemic. You may want to fact-check the science on that but I did *my research* about Covid-19 on the World Wide Web, wink wink.

Coronavirus was the ingredient no one wanted in their recipes. This bitter-tasting add-on was suddenly in everything. Wedding cakes with an arugula layer. Graduation dinners serving only broccoli. Baby births fuelled solely by orange peel.

You see, all my life I had lived with a healthy respect for recipes; risk was not my BFF. Recipes are really just rules that when followed make culinary delights, but for me, recipes are about more than just food. They are a guidebook for living a happy and secure life. If I don't follow the directions, all hell might break loose and I would feel frustrated, overwhelmed by choice, and cranky AF. I've never been a "just wing it" girl for the important meals. I'm allergic to risk. Risk exists in the spaces where you don't follow the recipe. I have always felt a special friendship with control, planning, and ensuring exactly thirty-seven chocolate chips go in the cookie batter.

This rule-following disposition was my genetic gift from my mother, Patsy. She, and her mother before her, were taught the importance of 'doing it right'. Right meant doing it the way you were told to do it. The way the recipe said. No exceptions. No substitutions. It was very important to my mom to give me all the ingredients I would need to ensure that my whipped shortbread cookie life would be melt-in-your-mouth delicious. Pretty sure Patsy's recipe did not include Coronavirus.

The sudden changes to my life's recipe were particularly annoying because 2019 had been probably the best year of my life. I was on a high. I celebrated fortieth birthdays (mine included), at spas, yoga camps, and restaurants in cities and tiny towns with life-long best friends. It was the year the Fritish man nervously balanced on one knee in public and asked me to be his wife. It was the year I finally got to plant my feet in England and see a part of the world beyond what my small-town eyes could imagine. I had tea with Liz at the palace. Fine, too far, I drank Starbucks outside the gates of Buckingham Palace, but to me all of this was like the most perfect fresh-baked bread. Warm, soul-satisfying, and full of carbs.

When the pandemic sliced and diced the ingredients for my future, I didn't slam the cookbook shut and stop roasting up plans. I didn't learn to knit, complete ten-thousand-piece puzzles, or Marie Kondo-roll all of the items in my drawers. Oh ya, I did do that last one, never mind. I wasn't going to sit on hold and see if the pandemic would stop playing elevator music and let me book a flight, have a party, or touch another human outside of my household without fear of being arrested or dying. Instead, I kept insisting that my life would go forward. I was going rogue, badass rule-breaker, that was me, insert eye roll.

I could still marry the man I had waited thirty-eight years to find, in my fancy frock. Sir Hadley James Winsby III, my fourteen-year-old pug, could still wear a tuxedo and be driven down the aisle in his child-sized remote-controlled sports car. I could have a socially distanced chilly outdoor picnic with personalised charcuterie boxes and tiny individual bottles of bubbly. I just had to embrace that my wedding cake would have store-bought icing instead of hand-whipped buttercream. I would be missing very important people I wanted to hug, eat with, dance with, and cry with. Let's be honest, it was probably best there was no open bar or open 'mic at my wedding.

Just before Dr. Bonnie flipped the closed sign on the public gathering door, we rocked a virtual elopement. I stood with the ocean behind me, my soon-to-be husband in front of me and a very small group of fascinator-wearing guests around us. We said "I do" to a life together while streaming the event to hundreds of friends and family across three continents. Exactly the same as William and Kate's wedding but totally different.

Okay, okay, a micro-wedding isn't exactly the definition of rogue badass rule-breaking. But wait, I haven't gotten to the good part. What the viewers of my big fat internet wedding did not know was that I was wearing two pairs of Spanx and had a gummy-bear sized best man in my tummy.

Fritish Man and I decided that one or two years were too precious to waste on a Covid pause and could mean the parenthood bus might pass us by. Seven weeks before the wedding, on my fiancé's forty-second birthday, I presented him with a plastic stick drenched in pee and the word YES. My friends say I give great gifts and I think this may have been my finest work.

My list of life goals did not include a geriatric pregnancy during a pandemic. Nowhere in my wildest dreams did I think that my friends and family would be out searching for toilet paper or locked in their homes while I experienced the magic of making a human with my body. That I would not have a picture of myself dramatically licking chocolate pudding out of a diaper at my baby shower. So many things I just assumed would happen, did not. Not a single stranger would admire how big my belly was, ask me when I was due, or any other potentially invasive questions. There would be no last getaway for me and my new husband to enjoy before we became a trio. Not a single best friend was going to hug me and place their hands on my belly and feel my baby show off his soccer skills. No one would come to visit us in the hospital.

But here's the thing. We were so happy and we were very, very grateful. I was healthy and pregnancy was very easy for me. Did I fall asleep at my desk? You bet I did. Did I pee my pants a couple of times? Correct. Was it pretty uncomfortable having a head smash against my ribs while doctors said the baby's position was all good, only to be told later, "Sorry my bad, this baby is super breech?" Totes. However, our pregnancy sandwich still had way more wonderful ingredients than shit.

I distinctly remember hearing that the menu for childbirth included almost dying from horrendous pain, screaming at the top of your lungs at Mr. Baby Daddy, "You did this to me!" and pooping on a table. Sounded pretty messed up if I'm being totally honest, but if that was the way it had to be, I was willing to do it. When I heard that my actual take-out order would instead include chopping my midsection open and evicting my tiny tenant, my first thought was a firm, *no thank you, I'd like to poop on the table, please.*

Here's the thing: that last-minute alteration in the program was the best substitute in my case. I finished work on Friday and went to the hospital first thing Monday morning, full term, to pick up my baby. I had an unplanned scheduled C-section and it was super slick. I walked to the operating room, they stabbed me with some crazy liquid causing half of my body to forget to feel pain, and less than twenty minutes later they handed me the cutest, cleanest hairless puppy anyone could hope for. Our sandwich was actually pretty delicious.

Coronavirus took things from me. Important things. Things that cannot be replaced. However, that jerk of a party-crashing virus gave me gifts too. It challenged me to find another way. To question what I really wanted and what was most important. It gave me a path to motherhood that I am not sure I would have otherwise taken. It confirmed that if you don't follow the exact recipe all hell will not automatically break loose. That letting go of control could actually feel amazing.

I have just arrived at motherhood. I am still trying to clear customs and locate my luggage. Life with a newborn is messy. The sleep deprivation and self-doubt are very real. There is no rule book. No best or right way. No one singular expert authority. Lack of control is super uncomfortable. Being a mother is the ultimate shit sandwich. Some moments there will be so much joy you think your heart will blow out of your chest and other moments will be awful and you will cry. Oh gawd, how you will cry. But if you can learn to love the shit, oh so much shit, you'll sit down to a five-star dinner every night.

Maybe I'll take my Fritish man and our Fritadian offspring to go stay in that castle for our anniversary. Maybe we'll have dessert, then dinner, then that appetizer. I am super flexible after all.

♥

Lana creates fun and laughter in any situation. She's an excellent gift-giver who speaks her own special dialect of Lananese which includes sayings from her family's Irish heritage and other made-up words. For example, "Ooga Dooga" is a sound/phrase used when lovingly squeezing her fourteen-year-old pug Sir Hadley James Winsby III, or her baby, her husband, or her bestie...Lana believes that a life without chips is not worth living. Hard to disagree.

here's your
PERMISSION SLIP:

to DRINK *the* COFFEE
to EAT *the* DONUT
to TAKE CHARGE
to REST
to take A NAP
to SAY YES

Digital Balloons

Baby showers haunted me. I dreaded every invite rattling chains in my inbox. Digital pink balloons and softly hued banners exclaiming, 'Oh Baby' in some jaunty font. Ominous. And I always thought the teddy bears in bow ties looked suspicious.

When Amanda's invitation popped up, it was no different; a diligent stork on her way to drop off a precious package to a new mother. For most people, the stork was a quaint icon. A symbol of the beginning of motherhood. To me, it was an overgrown pigeon who hadn't had proper training. If only it were that easy: place your order, mark it for air delivery and the shipping would be free.

Hovering the mouse over the Accept button...then the Decline button...and then the Maybe button, I didn't know what to do. In the end, I didn't respond at all. Eventually, I received a follow-up message from the host. I sent my apologies and tried to suppress my guilt on the day of the shower. I didn't have any other plans.

Amanda was family. Part of my large, extended blended family. And we all showed up. We showed up to birthdays and graduations, our annual costume party always had a new theme and my mom's house was always full. You couldn't tell the siblings from the step siblings, the partners from the cousins. We were all happy to see each other and be together. Of course, there were times when someone wasn't able to attend one of the many functions, but the reason was always clearly stated and the absentee was always missed. An unexplained absence at a baby shower would most certainly have been noted. But I just couldn't bring myself to play games with diaper pins and plastic babies and eat small sandwiches with the crusts cut off. I wanted to share in Amanda's excitement. I was genuinely happy for her. But I knew that if I opened up to her baby joy, I would also open up my own wound, which was deep and bled readily. Keeping it bandaged was a full-time job.

I had been waiting in the wings for so long. I was desperate for a shower of my own, with silly hats and frosted cupcakes.

I wanted my friends and family rallying around me with their glasses in the air. It had been almost four years since my first miscarriage. Four years since I first had the niggling feeling that the road to motherhood may not be as easy as they taught us in high school.

I vaguely remember that time right before I saw the fertility specialist. Like the moments between dreaming and waking; when I still felt warm and sweet and barely conscious. I had miscarried once, but the desire to bring my own child into the world had rushed back quickly and I was ready to try again. The loss had been great but I was certain the universe couldn't be so cruel as to let me go through that a second time. So I gleefully talked to my friends about all the things I would do once I was pregnant. I had baby names picked out and knew the top strollers of the year. Picking out fuzzy PJ's with feet and onesies with silly sayings, like "I'll have a bottle of the house white.' It was a dreamy sliver of time. I revelled in baby showers then. Before my shoulders started slumping from the weight of longing. Before the lines that mapped my face could be undone. Before the repeated disappointments that spiralled me into despair.

When I finally sat down with the fertility specialist, it was a harsh awakening, cold water in my face. I was dumbfounded and could barely grasp what the doctor had said. I understood that my body wasn't working the way it should. There was a blockage and a syndrome and it would be very hard for me to have a baby. There were going to be tests and procedures and a surgery; and then the IVF could start. But all I could hear was waiting, so much waiting. My baby was moving further and further away.

I turned to stone and then I crumbled. Wetness seeped from my eyes and drenched my cheeks. My husband leaned in and softened against me as he clutched my hand. I couldn't look at him. No words in my throat. I was knocked over; crushed into dust, waiting to be swept into the bin.

And so I couldn't go to another pastel party.

Late for brunch with my girlfriends one morning, I walked into a lively conversation about baby bedtime. Amelia slept the whole night through. Toby was up twice a night. Bella needed a bottle to sleep. As I sat and listened to the banter I thought I was smiling and nodding along but when one of my friends took my hand under the table and whispered, "Are you okay?" I realized my face had contorted into a squished-up mess.

I would have given anything to be able to contribute to a discussion about poo blowouts and toddler tantrums or newborn all-nighters and endless laundry. These mundane conversations evoked a visceral reaction in me. Jealousy, anger, sadness, and embarrassment churned and bubbled up inside of me, threatening to boil over. But I compressed and restrained and pushed them all down. Because soon it would be my turn to share something. I'd have to speak.

No, the first embryo transfer didn't work.

Yes, another miscarriage.

No, the first surgery didn't work.

Yes, I'm having a second surgery.

No, the third embryo transfer didn't take.

Yes, they found an antibody in my blood. Yes, it's causing miscarriages. Yes, I'll need another specialist, and then I'll need another.

One brunch became years of these kinds of updates. Not having a baby or a baby bump at any social gathering at thirty-eight years old made me stand out in the most conspicuous way. So I made myself invisible. A phantom who didn't show up to the baby showers anymore. And the brunch dates disappeared from my calendar, too. At family functions, I avoided Amanda and her new baby girl; if I had thought to wear beige pleather to blend into my mom's couch I would have.

Becoming a mother had always been a certainty. I was meant to be a mother. It was more than just my biological make up; hollow belly and curved breasts, born a blueprint for life. It felt deeper and destined. But my body had turned against me and the soft illusion of naturally becoming a mother was evaporating. And once that was gone, what was I left with? Who was I left with? I questioned my identity, right to the very core.

I felt unwomanly. If I couldn't carry a baby, who was I? Who was I, if I couldn't be a mother? I lived on the verge of screaming.

I would go as far as I had to. I allowed my body to be injected and sliced and stitched and scraped. Over and over. I popped pills and bled and cried from the pain. It was a slow, lonely trauma.

One day, after the second surgery on my fallopian tube, I got a message from an old friend. A woman I hadn't seen in a long time. It read, 'I wanted to check in on you. I know you're going through a hard time and I've been there. It can feel lonely but you're not alone. Let me know if you want to chat.' I blinked. I knew she had battled to conceive her own children. The compassion rushed through my body. And for a very brief moment, I did feel a little less lonely. A little less invisible. She saw me, and offered empathy, even though I was shutting myself off, even though I never went to her son's first birthday party, or to her daughter's.

Her simple gesture softened me enough to begin to see the warmth and community that were being offered from many people in my life. Old family friends would check in with my mom, genuinely asking how I was doing. An aunt I hadn't seen in a while, held my hands and told me to "keep having hope, you are going to be the best mother." Colleagues became confidants and kept their doors and arms open for me. And Amanda never begrudged my absence at her baby shower.

It was our turn to host Thanksgiving and the whole family was coming for turkey and pecan pie. We had a lot to be thankful for. It had been almost two years since Amanda's baby shower and she would have her little one in tow. This time would be different. This time I couldn't wait to kiss and cuddle that giggling, dribbling little girl. Because I had a secret to share. A happy secret that I had been keeping for the past few months. I was pregnant.

As we sat around the table, I announced our big news. There were beaming smiles and long, warm hugs and champagne popping all around. But it was Amanda's reaction that I remember the most clearly. She threw her arms around me, held me tight and when she pulled away, her eyes were glistening. I was caught off guard. It hadn't occurred to me that she was so invested in my journey especially when I had been so absent from hers. She had been quietly rooting for me, had been hoping for me, and was elated when I finally experienced success. I hadn't been there when it was her turn to share baby news and make baby plans, but there she was, moved to tears for me.

I was eight months pregnant at my own woodland-animal-themed shower and the joy was palpable. My mom's house was full again—barely any room to turn around. My closest friends and family had put together the most beautiful decorations, cupcakes, games, and endless trays of delicious things to eat. Women from many different avenues of my life were present...my friend who sent that first message, my aunt with the kind words, old family friends and colleagues, too. And Amanda was there, toddler on her knee, sitting on my mom's beige couch with the biggest grin.

Looking around at all those warm faces, I realized I had been brought into a circle. Women who knew that the journey to motherhood counted. I couldn't ask for anything more: full heart, full belly. A mixture of magic and science.

It had been a dark five years, mountainous and stormy. But I broach this topic openly now in the hopes that other women navigating a similar heavy-hearted path can feel some compassion in the chaos and solidarity in the sadness. To let them know what I now know: the sisterhood of motherhood starts long before you birth your child. There is always a mother who will hold your hand and hold your heart if you are in need. Looking back on my journey, what I remember the most are the women who travelled beside me. Who didn't give up on me. And although those years were painful, the memories that are the most vivid in my mind are those of the arms that wrapped around me along the way.

♥

In her downtime, Katie can be found strolling alongside the ocean or through the North Shore trails at a toddler's pace with her family. Katie is a passionate Special Education Teacher and cares deeply for her students and finding strengths in others. When she cranks up the music in her car, it is likely, "Let it Go," from Frozen...thanks to her daughter, the DJ. Exercise and slowing down with a chai tea latte are Katie's favourite "me time" moments.

Adina

♥

Milestones

A mixed bag of joy and shit in varying measures, milestones make us cheer and celebrate. They also trigger a tangle of painful emotions.

Mom, we have shared many memorable moments, like when you pulled me out of school to just hang out and cheer me up when I was feeling down, or when you handed me a bouquet of wildflowers at my long-awaited university graduation, and my wedding in the tiny chapel of Lions Gate Hospital. Just forty-eight hours prior, there hadn't even been an official engagement. It's amazing the miracles that happen when urgency is the driver.

What you didn't see were your palliative care doctors and nurses advising us to get married ASAP if we wanted you to be there. When I reflect, I think OMG they were so presumptuous! Clearly though, they recognized the love shared between me and my beloved, as well as our great love for you. Mom, you weren't privy to the hustle required to pull off our wedding. You didn't see the engagement in the bustling hospital cafeteria or the quickly made plans that followed. You weren't with me when I hurriedly found and bought my wedding dress off the rack in twenty minutes flat. You didn't see the delegation of tasks to relatives and close friends. Thankfully, you got to witness the main event. Just Hubs and me, poinsettias and winter blooms, and a tight circle of loved ones—and you in your wheelchair, breathing oxygen. One of the last milestones we would share.

"It's hard to lose a mom."

That's all the card said. In a sea of condolence messages, this one stood out. When I held the thick, smooth paper in my tired hands and read those words, I felt seen. Understood. All of my friends still had their moms. I was without. It was comforting to know someone else had already navigated this path and made it through. Hope.

About a decade later, with some healing and therapy under my belt, dear Hubs and I were expecting your first grandchild. As you may have expected, I felt fairly capable and figured the grieving process of being a motherless daughter was complete. I'd checked that off the list. Done!

I was wrong.

You see, Mom, I was actually adrift and unconsciously searching for a lost key I thought only you had. In prenatal classes, friends would jabber on about their own mother's experiences with pregnancy and childbirth and instead of sharing in their confident excitement, I felt distressed. I latched onto the notion that magic lay within family history. A history we didn't get the chance to talk about. The answers were beyond my reach.

Despite my dedication to personal development and spiritual growth, I fell into the common mom-to-be scheme of throwing oneself headlong into engineering an ideal pregnancy and crafting the perfect birth plan complete with a soothing playlist. I have to laugh at my cluelessness and how, of course, nothing went as planned. You would've been proud though. A+ for effort. You didn't raise a slacker.

Mom, why hadn't you prepared me by sharing your stories? Why didn't I ask critical Q's when I was in my early twenties? How were your pregnancies? Ever miscarried? Experience difficulty with fertility? Natural or drugs with childbirth? Labour times? Breastfed or formula? Also, a side note—what time was I born? I can't sort out my astrology or Human Design without this information because disappointingly, it's not available in any records. But really, I simply would've loved to hear more about my birth story and your experience around it. I longed to compare your stories with mine and to experience your loving care for a little longer. I imagined you showing me how to wrap my babies up tight with your quiet confidence. I pictured you dancing and rocking your grandbabies in your arms whilst singing nonsensical soothing songs.

"It's hard to lose a mom."

Congratulations, you're a mom! You have a daughter! You have a son! First smiles!—Oh wait, that's gas. Nevermind, we'll cheer anyhow. First steps, first day of kindy, first Christmas concert, first soccer goalie save, elementary school graduations, first day driving (OMG, now I understand why you put me straight into driving school), high school grad and entrance into uni. Your grandkids' milestones. We celebrate. And I grieve. There's a shadow. You are gone, but you're not. I see your kind, loving heart in your grandson. I see your old-soul wisdom in your granddaughter. Your smile is in their smiles. I wonder what it would've been like if my kids had known you, and you them.

"It's hard to lose a mom."

I remember when your mom died...my grandmother. I was three years old, and you took me to the Philippines. I remember you crying. When my brother and I graduated from high school, went to university and became more independent, were you proud and was it also bittersweet? Did you feel heartbroken when I moved out? When we forgot to call, did your stomach churn with worry? Then, I had no idea about heartstrings. Now I do. I wish I had known - I would've squeezed you harder.

"It's hard to lose a mom."

I wish you'd told me that grief isn't a "to-do" that can be checked off a list. It's a sneaky, biting reminder that keeps coming round when I least expect it. Instincts told me to run, run, RUN from the pain. And I would do exactly that, followed by a thorough berating for not being over it already. Suck it up. It's been years. What's wrong with you? Enough with the pity-party. On the flip side was the ever-popular coping strategy of toxic positivity. Everything is just grrrrreat! What I didn't know then is that welcoming the agonizing sorrow makes room for deeper healing.

"It's hard to lose a mom."

Nine years after that tiny wedding, and your passing, I was pregnant and still grieving you. I didn't have the clarity to name it. Instead, I felt invisible, alone and weak, with a profound sense of longing for words of validation and acceptance. All along what I really needed to hear was, "Of course, you're missing your mom. Obviously, you feel sad. It sucks! Your feelings are legit. Nothing's wrong with you."

Alas, much of the time the children were small I was barely keeping it together. Hubs travelled five days a week in those early years and I didn't have the capacity for self-reflection. How could I grieve you while juggling the daily joys and demands of early motherhood largely alone? My world was full with disjointed sleep rhythms, sweet smiles, not-so-sweet diapers, weird rashes, mashed bananas, giggles and tears, and questioning the wisdom of countless parental decisions like crying-it-out or continued co-sleeping.

"It's hard to lose a mom."

I was caught off-guard by the hot jealousy that ripped through my body when friends referenced their mothers during after-school chatter..."Just dropping the kids off at Mom's"..."Mom's coming to stay and watch the kids while we jet off to Palm Springs"..."Mom sent a care package—isn't this outfit adorable?!!"..."I took Mom's advice and let her cry"..."My mom is so bossy"..."I was feeling overwhelmed, so I called my mom"...Blah, blah, blah blah...STOP! I didn't want to hear it! I would stuff down my jealousy, labelling it as bad and unevolved. How dare I have ugly feelings? Mature, well-adjusted people don't feel this way. Get a grip.

"It's hard to lose a mom."

It's been twenty-eight years since you transitioned, Mom, and thankfully that mixed bag is more full of joy than sadness. The sharp edges of grief have softened and I can no longer remember the sound of your voice. Today, we share another milestone. I am now the same age you were when you died. Hubs and I shared a bottle of wine and a home-cooked meal, and the kids sang happy birthday to me. It feels momentous and even a little rebellious. I will live beyond your years.

Now that I have the perspective of time, I realize I've always been the holder of the key. Intuition is my guide. And, as you'd promised before you died, an abundance of nurturing mother energy surrounds me in the form of spirit, my guides, aunties, a mother-in-law, your son—my brother, a sister-in-law, loyal friends, and even in the kindness of strangers sharing encouraging words like, "It's OK...You're OK." You've got this.

While no one can ever replace you, you live on in me and through your grandkids.

One day, my children will be without me and I hope they take heart and give themselves some grace. I have faith they will allow their feelings to surface and create space for grief and the wisdom that inevitably follows.

"It's hard to lose a mom."

For now, I get to regale your grandkids with family stories and their history. While I'm often met with puzzled stares or even eye rolls, your grandson knows all about when he was born. Your granddaughter knows how my pregnancies went and when perimenopause kicked in. Your grandchildren know how you loved to sing at your church and how you were a doctor and nurturing person—and how friends and family would flock to you for counsel. You were everyone's best friend. My kids both know how Hubs and I rushed to plan and hold our wedding in that small hospital chapel, so you could be there with us. Mom, your grandchildren know you through stories and I like to think they also feel your loving presence—just like I do.

♥

Adina is an introvert who sings '80s tunes in her car. She likes to remind people to "listen to the whispers—what is your intuition telling you?" The whispers often tell her to snuggle up with her two French bulldogs and a juicy book, ideally somewhere hot with a beach and a pool. Her monkey mind and the weight of the world may occasionally distract Adina but her optimism and cheerleader's heart, along with her four-step skincare regimen, keep her smiling.

Ashley

Great Boots / Bad Blood

In October 2010, while packing up Thanksgiving leftovers, I dropped an empty Tupperware container and it bruised my entire foot. I have bruised easily all of my life; it's a long-running joke. I once had bruised elbows from leaning on a desk.

At six and a half months pregnant, I felt like absolute garbage. Just walking and grocery shopping were extremely challenging. One flight of stairs felt like running a marathon. Since I wasn't going anywhere fast and retail therapy is a thing, I treated myself to some very outlandish and expensive boots from John Fleuvog. They had a pirate feel to them, rich jewel-toned green with a wide brown leather folded top and a chunky wooden sole. I wore them as often as I could.

After walking what should have been an easy four blocks to my midwife's office for my thirty-three-week check-up, I collapsed, sweaty and exhausted, on the examination bed with the grace of a manatee. I was, of course, wearing my incredible boots, which my midwife immediately complimented. She is also a woman of eccentric tastes so I was pleased she liked them and thanked her, but also pointed out the rash they had been giving me.

After examining the rash and the ridiculous bruise on my foot she suggested a blood test was in order.

After a lovely lunch hour walk on the seawall where I mostly sat on a variety of benches, and a quick visit to the lab for blood work, I arrived home and started preparing dinner—that night's meal specifically designed to maximize my iron intake which I felt was the cause of my extreme fatigue.

The phone rang at 4:45 p.m. A voice on the other end explained I needed to get to the hospital. Right away. My blood levels were critically low—my life and the baby's were in critical danger.

We rushed directly to the maternity ward. My blood was tested again and I was quickly given a series of blood transfusions. That evening I learned my bone marrow was failing. It couldn't produce the cells my body needed. I had virtually no immune system. My hemoglobin was so low I could have fainted and fallen over at any moment, and if that had happened there was an extraordinarily high likelihood of bleeding to death due to my blood's inability to clot. The rash on my legs was in fact the result of tiny blood vessels bursting, which had probably been caused by my swollen pregnant legs being shoved into those glorious boots.

A bone marrow biopsy was needed to accurately diagnose what was happening but regardless it was clear that I could not safely carry on with the pregnancy. The biopsy was performed that evening and my husband, Scott, and I began the agonizing wait for the results while our friends and family held vigil in the maternity waiting room.

Over the next two harrowing days, we planned for the baby's delivery, keeping my blood counts as high as possible through transfusions, and fasting in case we were given the go-ahead for a C-section. We finally received a diagnosis of Severe Aplastic Anemia (SAA). SAA is an ultra-rare auto-immune disorder that causes pancytopenic bone marrow failure which, if not treated, is fatal. Basically, my immune system was attacking my bone marrow. I was unable to produce mature red blood cells, platelets, white blood cells, or neutrophils. By ultra-rare I mean SAA is diagnosed in 2.5/1,000,000 people. In 2010 I was one of five people diagnosed with it in BC. It is most commonly seen in children or older people; rarely in my age group and even more rarely in a pregnant person. In other words, I am a unicorn.

Things moved quickly. I needed to have a platelet count over 80 in order to be approved for surgery. Platelets are what cause blood to clot and typical levels in a healthy human are between 150-400. When I was admitted to the hospital my platelet count was six. The C-section was scheduled for 7 p.m. and throughout the day I received platelets and red cell transfusions. If we couldn't get my platelets to 80, the baby would need to be delivered through surgery, under general anesthetic.

At 7 p.m., with a platelet count of 85, we got the go-ahead and our baby boy was born with me alert, and my husband and our midwife present. Our sweet little boy weighed four pounds fifteen ounces and was born one day shy of thirty-four weeks term. He was (and still is) perfect in every way. His little lungs needed some help so he was placed in an incubator and tucked safely away in the NICU to grow stronger.

Later that evening, we were told *my* treatment would not be able to take place at Lions Gate. The only hospital in the province that could treat *me* was Vancouver General Hospital (VGH) which has no maternity program. VGH was also 40 minutes and two bridges away. Cohen and I would be separated as soon as a bed at VGH's Leukemia and Bone Marrow Transplant ward was available. No one could tell me how long I would be there.

Four days later, when I was transferred, it felt like my soul ripped in half.

I arrived at 9 p.m. and was promptly taken to the Leukemia and Bone Marrow Transplant ward where twenty-five vials of blood were drawn. The doctors couldn't tell me what caused my SAA (idiopathic). It can sometimes appear in pregnancy but typically corrects itself postnatally (not in my case). I was warned that I was critically immunecompromised. In the coming days I would have a catheter inserted into my chest (called a Hickman Line) to deliver the life-saving blood and drugs I needed. My twin sister would undergo HLA testing to see if she was a bone marrow match (she wasn't) and I would need to have another biopsy.

The following morning my diagnosis was confirmed and I underwent several more tests and scans to ensure my body could handle what was to come. The plan was to try an immunosuppressive chemotherapy regimen intended to kick the hell out of my immune system. Essentially, we were hitting Ctrl-Alt-Del on my bone marrow by injecting me with a chemotherapy serum derived from the thymus gland of a horse...if the horse serum (Antithymocyte Globulin Equine) didn't work we would try ATG-Rabbit...science is amazing and so very, very weird.

The Hickman Line was inserted the next morning. I was terrified to turn my head or reach for anything in fear of tearing the uncomfortable stitches that held it in place while my skin healed. The line was needed because the chemo is so toxic it would burn my veins if administered intravenously...vein burning should definitely be avoided.

A subcutaneous test was done to determine how I may react to the chemo—an early warning system for the medical team. Judging by the large rash that formed on my arm, this was going to be very, very hard. With no other options, and considering how severely ill I was, we had to go ahead with the treatment. I was completely overwhelmed by all that was happening. Angry that I wasn't having the post-natal experience I expected, terrified I was going to die, and bargaining with the spirit world to just let me live long enough that my son would know and remember me.

During the day, while Scott was at work, our families took up NICU duty cuddling, feeding, bathing, and changing Cohen, or stayed with me supplying me with coffee, snacks, good meals, and company. Everyone was exhausted, terrified, and emotionally drained.

In the best-case scenario, if I responded well to the chemo, I could go home within two weeks. Worst-case scenario would require a bone marrow transplant from an unrelated donor and up to three months in hospital.

The day before my chemo started, and four days after arriving at VGH, I was given a day pass to go see our little boy. That visit, where I held my tiny boy and felt his fierce little heart, gave me every reason I needed to fight through what was to come. I spent several hours nursing him (once chemo started I could no longer breastfeed) and singing to him, I took pictures, and examined every inch of his platinum curly hair, bright blue eyes, and teeny tiny toes.

I got caught up on Cohen's progress by the nursing team who, upon learning I was a preemie twin delivered at the same hospital in 1979, looked up my birth records and noted that I was also born at about thirty-four weeks! I had thrived and I knew then that Cohen was going to be totally fine!

Chemo started the next morning. Twelve hours per day for four days straight. It went as badly as predicted. In order to manage my severe reactions to the drugs (rigors from fevers, hives all over, and severe shortness of breath) I was given oxygen, required steroids and antihistamines through my port constantly, and the transfusion rate was slowed to sixteen hours a day.

My memory of those four days is murky: I remember feeling incredibly cold and being unable to get warm, I remember struggling to catch my breath and that the medication blurred my vision so badly I thought I was going blind, I remember wondering if I was going to survive and feeling grateful that Cohen had Scott and he would always be cared for and loved.

The treatment, although incredibly taxing and slow, worked well. I was placed on immunosuppressive medications and monitored for a few days to see how I reacted. They gave me terrible nausea and had unpleasant side effects such as kidney dysfunction, weight gain, unwanted hair growth, and tremors, but they kept my immune system at bay. After nearly four weeks in the hospital I was finally allowed to go home.

We brought Cohen home two days later.

At home we tried to pretend things were normal. We were sleep-deprived parents to a newborn going through the motions of feed, play, bathe, sleep. I still had unbearable fatigue from low red blood cell counts; serum sickness from chemo that caused night sweats that soaked the mattress; and I was on enough medication to fill a cereal bowl. I also had to manage a rigorous outpatient regimen of daily trips to VGH's Bone Marrow Transplant Daycare. These appointments could last anywhere from two to eight hours. If I arrived and my blood counts were okay, I would be done in two hours. More often though, I would require platelets, red blood cells, and antibiotic infusions, and I would be there all day.

Over the next ten months, I slowly recovered, was declared in remission, came off all my medications and eventually returned to work. When Cohen was three years old I relapsed, returned to hospital, and did it all again, which was even harder. My reactions to the chemo horse serum were more severe, my recovery was slower, and now I had a toddler who loved to be carried everywhere and was curious about tugging at my Hickman Line. Again, Scott and I got through it together with the incredible support of our families.

Today, although I remain on immunosuppressive therapy in order to prevent another relapse (because of my unicorn status, I am one of very few SAA patients who are unable to come off medications following a return to normal blood levels), I don't let SAA slow me down. I enjoy life to the fullest, cherishing my family and friends and pursuing interests that fill my cup. And although my fashion sense is lacking these days, I still love those John Fleuvog boots—they literally saved my life.

♥

Work thoughts and mom guilt keep Ashley up at night. She was a high school theatre nerd and folk music fan who still sings sea shanties in the shower. She decompresses on her spin bike or with a hike in the forest. As the Executive Director of Howe Sound Women's Centre, Ashley is passionate about eliminating gender-based violence and fighting for equality from an intersectional feminist lens. Do not mumble in her presence.

@ASHLEYSTOAKES

here's your
PERMISSION SLIP:

to GO *for a* WALK
to TAKE *a* TIME-OUT
to DRINK *wine with* GIRLFRIENDS
to KNOW *you're* AWESOME
to ORDER *take-out*
to PLAY

Paige

♥

Divergent

I stared at the test results on my phone feeling utterly frozen. My breath was shallow as shock and realization hit me. It was like in the flash of a moment, everything made sense.

Four years earlier, my reproductive psychiatrist had prescribed a nice little cocktail of anti-anxiety medication. At thirty-seven weeks pregnant with my first son, I had taken the obsession with nesting to a whole new level. There were sleepless nights spent meticulously organizing the freezer, a several-thousand-dollar overhaul made to our garage storage solutions, and hours spent collapsed on the floor agonizing over nursery design decisions. I experienced near-panic attacks just by walking into Babies-R-Us.

I looked to the side of the room, avoiding eye contact with my psychiatrist while I pretended to think clearly through her recommendation. With a deep breath, I declined the meds. Chalk it up to anxiety about the possible side effects for the baby (*oh, the irony*). Besides, this wasn't my first rodeo when it came to mental health. I could probably teach the workshop on cognitive behavioural therapy, counsel you through the ten unhelpful thinking styles, and recite the benefits of mindfulness all day long. Hell, this wasn't even the first time I had straight-up refused medication. I'd been here before, many times.

Anxiety and depression have pretty much ruled the greater portion of my life. I developed my first eating disorder at age twelve. When puberty hit, so did a sense of negative body image, and I took an interest in diet and nutrition. Researching everything I could about healthy eating and exercise, the more I learned, the more restrictive I became. This insatiable sense of control over my existence quickly became an obsession. Before I knew it, I weighed seventy pounds and was put into treatment for anorexia.

Even as a young child, my focus and determination controlled me. Little interests would easily consume my thoughts. I was named the perfectionist in my family, spending painstaking hours completing grade school homework. A simple poster project would spiral hard and fast into a pilgrimage for perfection. You'd find me spread out on the kitchen table carefully colouring in all the provinces on the map as if I were Picasso. Most of the time my family thought I was downright crazy, but in my mind, they just didn't understand the gravity of my assignment. I mean, it was the MAP. OF. CANADA.

It's easy now to poke fun at those seemingly innocent childhood quirks, but the reality of perfectionism continued to haunt me well beyond adolescence. As my commitments and responsibilities grew, so did a life-controlling need to achieve success at every level. My self-worth depended on being the best. My work ethic and determination were iron-clad. I would easily sacrifice friendships that got in the way; like leaving everyone behind to transfer high schools at the offer to join the national champion cheerleading team. The prestige of that uniform made me blind to everything else.

Eventually, I lost the strength to keep up with my own unattainable standards (*being human, ya know?*). School subjects got harder and I wasn't the smartest in every class anymore. I was named captain of the cheerleading team, but failed to be the leader I always thought I'd be. My signature fashion sense was buried in a new wardrobe of baggy sweats. I went from being the popular girl in school to a wandering outsider. I certainly wouldn't be giving the valedictorian speech I always thought I'd be a shoo-in for.

The weight of my shortcomings crushed me. I fell into depression, spending entire days in bed sleeping to escape my inner reality of not being enough. Weeks, months, years spent head down, avoiding the world, doing everything I could to be invisible. I felt overwhelmed by expectations I couldn't live up to. A soul-piercing sense of shame and inadequacy covered me. The safest place to be was unseen.

I hit rock bottom at age seventeen, just a few months before graduating high school. I couldn't stop time or escape the spinning world. Hopelessness overtook me. I was trapped in my pain and ready to end it all. By the grace of God, I didn't. Instead, that fateful experience turned into a cry for help. My darkness was shattered by a tiny army of real-life guardian angels, blowing up my phone with desperate concern. My sister, an ex-boyfriend, a couple of co-workers, and eventually my mom. Together, they carried me out of isolation and into the world of facing my mental-health demons head-on.

The path towards healing was not linear—more like a maze with hidden dead-ends, secret U-turns, and finish lines that were really just the beginning. The cycle of striving hard to prove I was worth something, and always coming up short, went on for years. Bouncing around to different counsellors, therapists and doctors, I received all kinds of diagnoses: depression, anxiety, disordered eating, chronic fatigue, fibromyalgia, endometriosis, hyperalgesia, premenstrual dysphoric disorder...to name a few. I've spent years reading books, journalling, talking to professionals, and doing the self-work. I've untangled childhood trauma and unlearned misguided core beliefs.

Falling in love with my husband showed me for the first time what unconditional love and belonging felt like. I came to terms with the fact that my perfectionism had nothing to do with striving for my best, and everything to do with a deep fear of not being accepted as I am. While I'm damn proud of the work I've done to overcome my shit, I've also spent a lot of time contemplating an awareness that there are certain things about me I'll never change. Traits that are hardwired in me, and fundamental parts of who I am.

No matter how I slice it, my capacity to juggle simultaneous demands is painfully small. I tend to see details that other people miss, and when I'm passionate about something, there's no possibility of breaking my determination. I gravitate towards predictability, and being faced with unfamiliar situations puts me on edge. Furniture with efficient functionality sparks joy like you wouldn't imagine. Freedom over my schedule is non-negotiable, and I thrive when I make my own rules. Clutter and chaos make my chest tight and mind foggy, and nothing stresses me out like impending small talk. When I'm in the zone, I can build an online business in five days flat, but I'll forget daycare pick-up while I'm at it. I'm a fearless dreamer, but sharing my grandest vision with other people terrifies me.

These tendencies have been the driving force behind much of my life's evolution. They've knocked me down and held me back in many ways, while at the same time, they've led to most of my greatest accomplishments. They were the reason I dropped out of university halfway through, feeling unable to balance the course load and overwhelmed by the list of credits. They also account for how I've lived my entire adult life with no trace of a budget while reaching all my financial goals through sheer will. I've quit every full-time job I've ever had because I felt like I had better things to do than live by corporate rules. I self-taught my way to professional-level skills in all kinds of creative and technical fields—videography, graphic design, and more. I built an industry-leading business, plus a few side hustles, because I found my passion in entrepreneurship. I've produced hundreds of flawless high-profile events because there's no detail or set of logistics that can escape my claws. For better or worse, these characteristics have defined my life. Through years of self-work, I've tried to learn to honour my limits and harness my energy for the best, though I've fallen flat on my face more times than not.

Remember that medication I willfully declined at nine months pregnant? Five weeks after my son was born, I surrendered to the pills. I was a mother now. It was no longer just about my own well-being; it was about my son's. Plus, postpartum hormones are no joke.

Truthfully, I started to fear those intrinsic traits of mine. I knew all too well the reality of growing up with parents emotionally entangled in their own anxiety and control issues. I experienced first-hand how that rigid and critical authority over a kid's life can shatter their self-worth. How the pattern of invalidating feelings and perceptions in the most fragile developmental years breeds emotional trauma that stays with them for life. I knew the painful of counselling sessions spent unravelling belief systems ingrained in me long before I had the maturity or wisdom to know any different. I'd be damned if I'd let my son experience what I did, or anything close to it.

The meds were life-changing. That extra boost of serotonin melted away layers of baggage that had smothered my wild and free soul. My brain understood my mind better, and my mind took the crisis level down a few notches. I settled into motherhood with a newfound sense of balance and self-awareness, or so I thought.

Perhaps in some ways, the clarity made it easier for me to work harder. As I found my footing in this new season of life, my default tenacious ways manifested full-tilt in being a working mom and female business leader. I hustled harder than ever, moving the goalpost along as I reached every achievement I set my mind to. By the time we welcomed our second son, I had grown into somewhat of a workaholic. A few short weeks after giving birth, I returned to work full-time. Without even realizing the path I was on, I had fallen back into the clutches of my mental-health demons. Or maybe these were just the things about me I would never change. Whatever the case, I had no time or energy to figure it out. I was busy, confused, and very tired.

That's when our oldest son was diagnosed with autism. Squeezed in between meetings, feedings, and a steady stream of work emails, I sat with the psychologist as my beautiful three-year-old boy paced back and forth on his tippy-toes, tapping his fingers on every surface in the room like a drum. "He will receive an autism diagnosis, I think you're prepared for that," she said to me.

Oh right, yeah...wait, was I prepared for it? I mean, kind of. We'd been considering the possibility for the last year or so, and had read up about ASD when his pediatrician made the assessment referral. Still, nothing could've prepared me for the path of discovery I was heading down.

As any mother would do, I made it my mission to understand his challenges and the type of help he needed to be his best self. I quickly learned about the movement to accept neurodiversity. That autism isn't something to be fixed or cured, but rather just a different way of being human; how people on the spectrum experience the world differently, and that will never change for them.

Sadness set in when I realized my son would have to grow up in a world that was stacked against him. He's brilliant and creative and talented, but the structures of our society would make it harder for him to shine. He would need to pave his own way, learning and living on his own terms. Also, I would drop-kick any kid, teacher, or parent who makes him feel inadequate or unaccepted for who he is.

The more I processed the challenges he might face, the more connected I felt to him. I started to realize that my own experiences weren't that different. I related to what I was reading about his sensory processing sensitivities, and the suffering he was trying to express through misunderstood behaviours. Even when my husband couldn't make sense of his attempts to communicate, he made sense to me. I recognized myself in the way he was.

The way Disneyland makes him cranky and defiant is the same way a chaotic family dinner with loud cross-talk makes me irritable and disengaged.

The way he paces back and forth during play dates is the same way I fidget with my hands in business meetings.

The way he gets mad when you mess with his puzzle pieces is the same way I snap at the sound of my phone ringing when it interrupts my train of thought.

The way he demands we turn off extra noise when he's piecing together an idea is the same way I can't text and listen to a conversation at the same time.

The way he needs extra time to mentally prepare for an outing to the playground is the same way I'm a dysfunctional human when my quiet hour of coffee in the morning is disturbed.

The way he relies on predictability to feel at ease and loses the ability to cope effectively when he's beyond his capacity, is me.

It started to dawn on me that his neurodivergent nature could maybe be mine too. Swift denial pushed right back on that idea. There was no way I could be autistic. I was thirty-two years old. Everyone knew me as successful, bubbly, and full of ambition. I mean, sure, maybe my eye contact wasn't the greatest, but I had learned to improve that in the professional world. Instinctively I kind of hated social gatherings with people I didn't know, but I considered myself an extrovert once I was at the party. Okay, I didn't have any close friends besides family, but that was only because I was really busy. I had no problem connecting emotionally with people when I wanted to, it's just that maintaining close friendships was exhausting, so I chose to love people from a safe distance. And yes, my sister did earnestly endorse the peculiar fact that I'd been overwhelmed since grade three, but...well, I didn't really have a good explanation for that one.

Confusion and curiosity kept me Googling. I read about the concept of "masking" in autistic people. I learned that women have a much higher ability to camouflage their autistic traits and adapt to social demands. The idea of the female phenotype of autism was a fast-emerging area of research and was showing that girls with high intellectual abilities were very likely to go undiagnosed. Diagnostic measures were skewed towards boys, and misperceptions of the condition among medical professionals caused autistic girls to slip through the cracks.

That was fascinating and all, but there still was no way I could actually be autistic. This push and pull between utter denial and undeniable facts spun me into an identity crisis. I pondered my childhood experiences as I walked daily through many similar ones with my son. From delayed potty training to extreme aversions to certain types of clothing, I wondered whether my son just wasn't *that* autistic, or whether I was. I Googled phrases like, "are eating disorders a symptom of autism in girls," and "can autistic people be emotionally intelligent?" Stumbling around the internet for answers, I came upon a Canadian psychologist who had been diagnosed with autism herself at forty-two years old. She had created a practice to help adults, like herself, gain the self-understanding, validation, and acceptance that comes with an autism diagnosis. A diagnosis that's nearly impossible for adults to access, and for which there's no standardized assessment to administer to anyone over the age of nineteen.

Consumed by her library of resources, I clicked a link in one of the articles that took me to a screening tool for measuring social camouflaging behaviours in adults. According to the article, it was a crucial test to help identify "hidden" autism in the highly intelligent female type.

I started the questionnaire. Reading each statement carefully, my responses were strikingly obvious. The scenarios described in the test were uncanny; like reading my life. Some of them were such an accurate picture of my quirks, it made me laugh out loud.

The results came back consistent with the prevalence of autism spectrum disorder.

The revelation sank in as I scrolled through the report, section by section. My mind struggled to comprehend it, but the truth was relentless. The simplest explanation for everything about me that had been so complicated.

I spent weeks quietly processing and reflecting over every piece of the way I am. I continued with further screening, and connected with the autistic adults community. I engaged in conversations with researchers and psychologists who specialized in diagnosis for adults like me. Through the process of shock, realization and acceptance, my identity crisis slowly melted away.

I am neurodivergent; a fancy way of saying I'm on the spectrum. Yes, I'm autistic. Though I struggle with some weird feeling of imposter syndrome about this label, I also find it profoundly validating. As if suddenly I have a clinical hall pass to embrace the way I am. Being easily overwhelmed or prone to perfectionism isn't a sign of weakness or inadequacy, it's part of my neurological disposition. It's the way my brain is wired to operate.

In the midst of this newfound enlightenment and freedom to be myself, I arrived at the *real* epiphany. Why did I need a diagnosis to grant me permission to be fully the person I was created to be? Nothing about me had changed. I'd been existing this way my entire life. Only now, with the endorsement of some scientists about having a thing, it seemed okay.

If you hear anything from my story, hear this. Every person born into this world has the authority to be unapologetically who they are; no matter what any society, doctor, parent, or opinion says about them.

I thought becoming a mother meant I would bestow wisdom upon my children from the years of life I'd lived before them. I was wrong. My son has already taught me more about life than I will ever teach him.

Paige is a hazard until she's had her morning coffee. To unwind she loves a book, a cozy blanket, and some calm acoustic music, though with two young boys, downtime looks more like Blue's Clues, couch forts, and wailing toddler jams. Paige's superpower is being too strong-willed to give up on her dreams; whether that means building a business or mastering a performance of her favourite rap song. Her alter ego is DJ Pajmina on Spotify and her playlists are legendary.

♥

The Light Side of Dark

I know where every bathroom is.

That might be a bit of an exaggeration. Let me clarify. I know where every bathroom is in every place I have ever visited. I've been to approximately ninety-eight cities in twelve countries. Yes. That is a LOT of fuckin' bathrooms. It's not like I have some weird fascination with bathrooms. In fact, I quite dislike most bathrooms—especially the ones "on the road."

This bathroom knowledge is a necessity. Those little tiled cubicles are my refuge. I cannot leave the house without knowing where every possible stop is. Why? To escape the sudden onset of cold shivers, the tightening of my chest, and constriction of my throat. Explosive diarrhea accompanied by volcanoes of vomit and the desperate choking for air, then the resulting humiliation when emergency services are called to peel my near-lifeless body from the side of the road while my kids look on in horror. Has this scenario ever happened? No. Of course not. Welcome to the wonderful world of anxiety. And the terrifying feeling of being out of control.

I was diagnosed with a generalized anxiety disorder with panic attacks in my very late teens. It was a relief to know there was a name for what I grew up knowing only as "funny feelings."

I'm pretty open when it comes to my struggles with anxiety—surface-level open, if I'm being completely truthful. Happy to share facts, statistics, and resources—the useful effects of therapy and medication. I will share that I have "suffered," although few people know what that truly means. Somewhere along the way, I learned to become an amazing "masker"—I believe this is the clinical term for liar.

Even those in my closest circle do not know the extent of my anguish. They don't know that I can't leave the house for days at a time while I sit in a ball in my bed paralyzed with fear, sweaty, shaky hands clutching my soft purple comforter and unable to speak, contemplating whether my place on this planet is worthwhile. They don't know I have been unable to sustain basic life function without excruciating effort. They don't know that it can take me upwards of an hour to put on a shirt or socks in the morning because the fabric needs to *feel* just so, and they certainly don't know that I once stopped eating for a year.

When I was six years old I choked on an egg roll. I can still remember the beansprouts dangling in my throat, and desperately gasping for air. I remember the panic. After that, I stopped eating. My parents presented my absolute favorite foods—burgers, french fries, pizza. They took me to my favorite restaurants, offered me ice cream for breakfast, begged and pleaded with me to "just try a bit" of some baby food—they were scared and desperate. I was more scared.

I. Ate. Nothing.

As I became more and more frail, I remember visiting the hospital many times with my family, seeing a person who must have been a psychiatrist. The rest is foggy. I don't actually know what kept me alive.

I could not have imagined the helpless terror my parents must have felt, until I saw my precious firstborn beginning to unravel. Watching on as my gorgeous son struggled to sleep alone, unable to fall asleep with the racing thoughts in his head telling him lies, obsessing over how clothing felt, unable to go to school because of stomach pain...he was classically me.

I will not tell his story, it's not mine to tell—but I can tell you that witnessing him suffer is every bit as heartbreaking and gut-wrenching as you might imagine.

There is a known nature and nurture component to anxiety, so as much as I worked to dampen the effects of my own illness on my innocent, perfect child, I failed. Now there it is. Fear and inner torment, staring back at me in the form of gorgeous, giant, baby-blue eyes. It hurts every day knowing that he shares my darkest side. I am consumed with sadness, guilt, and you guessed it...anxiety.

Despite our challenges, both my son and I have managed to perfect our facades of happiness and calm. Somewhere along the way I developed a sense of humour as a defense mechanism. It is generally easier to be the one to start the joke than to be the recipient of unsolicited mockery. In fact, I often have inner battles with myself over who the "real me" actually is. Monthly sessions with my therapist involve trying to distinguish this—only to ultimately acknowledge that it's okay to be me, with the darkness and the laughter.

Anxiety is a *part* of me, but it does not have to *define* me. When I feel the cold sweat begin, my heart beating faster, and my throat tightening, I continue to fight. It's exhausting—but the battle is necessary. Luke Skywalker needed to battle the darkness within him to salvage the universe, and now I must too. It is essential that I prove to my son that it is possible for light to coexist with the darkness.

"He *did* WHAT?!"

One week into taking a job as the district's specialist teacher in a program to support learners with mental health and behavioural challenges I receive a phone call from my son's teacher telling me that he has mooned the kids in his kindergarten class.

"Andrew, we need to talk about what happened today. Your teacher told us that you showed your bottom to your classmates at circle time. Why did you do that?"

"Well..." He started thoughtfully, "I didn't show them my penis. That would be inappropriate."

Having anxiety is so, so hard, but without my nasty wingman, I wouldn't be me; I wouldn't have accomplished the things I have. The more I learned how to dance with anxiety, the more I was drawn to working with people who were also jumping mental-health hurdles. I felt a kinship in particular with children. I became a teacher and specialized in working with students with mental health and behaviour challenges. My illness has been a huge asset to my work—it has drawn me toward an incredibly challenging population that I can understand and empathize with, and has given me tools and strategies to predict their explosive behavior, and know how to respond. After all, people with anxiety are always expecting the worst-case scenario, so when it happens, it doesn't come as a surprise to me—I had it all mapped out, along with a minimum of seven of the most appropriate responses. It is a bit of a superpower that way.

I have had students bring weapons to class, students who have experienced violent psychotic breaks, and students who engage in aggressive and toxic language regularly. Sometimes, that's one kid in one day! Who knew that working in a high-stress situation would be the perfect place for a person with high stress?!

It has taken a long time and a lot of therapy to come to the conclusion that I'm good at my job. To get over the imposter syndrome and realize that I AM an amazing educator. Being asked to present at workshops, being touted by colleagues for my amazing work, but not being able to get it right at home, stings. I continue to work on the belief that I am a good mom, but there is so much difficulty and pain when my son calls for "Daddy" every time he's upset. He doesn't want Mommy. But, just like me, he needs the co-regulation of a stable, calm presence. I can't blame him for this. As a child, he's still learning and trying to figure out how best to calm himself. I constantly feel as though I am falling short for him, not being the parent who is fully able to comfort and soothe him.

I gave my kids the best father on the planet. My husband is down-to-earth, calm, and thoughtful. When I'm anxious I have a tendency to check out, get short-tempered, frantically over-ask questions—or sometimes all of the above at once. He tells me I'm funny, thoughtful, kind, and beautiful almost everyday. Damn, I'm lucky. Like, lying in a patch of four-leaf clovers, tightly holding onto horseshoes whilst munching Lucky Charms, lucky.

My son has developed the same outlandish, coping sense of humour. We have come to realize that we are two peas in a little worry-filled pod. I want Andrew to know that anxiety isn't funny—except when it is. That we can always work to coexist with the fear and anguish within. Even the shittiest cup of coffee is drinkable with enough sugar in it. We can choose how to play the cards we're dealt in life. As humans, we all have something—shit, if you aren't suffering with something then THAT's what actually makes you weird. We need to embrace our afflictions and move forward with grace and a bit of humour.

> Me: *Uh, Andrew, honey, it looks like you need to do another flush.*
>
> A: *Why?*
>
> Me: *You left behind some poo.*
>
> A: *Mooooom...they're called* THE SURVIVORS! *But fine, I'll flush again.*

Truth be told, I have never grown out of my appreciation for immature humour. A quick-witted rude joke is right up there with a perfectly timed toot that loudly reverberates off the seat of a leather chair—there's really nothing better. As an adult, I have learned to rein in my reaction to such glorious hilarity. Unfortunately, it would seem as though we had some work to do with the little boy who has, for better or for worse, inherited my appreciation for such shenanigans. If I have simply passed along my sense of humour, as inappropriate and immature as it can be, and the ability to see the light in the darkness, that's a pretty huge fucking win. I mean, if you're going to pass along a debilitating mental illness, the least you could do is also set your kids up with the armour of a quirky sense of humour and uproarious laughter.

While pulling up to an American sporting goods store, Andrew and I both started to giggle. My husband Dan tossed us both a disapproving side eye and said, "Regan, don't encourage this." Andrew and I giggled a little harder, both trying desperately to contain our "inappropriateness."

> *"Come on, Dan," I said, "who names a store Dick's and doesn't expect a little laughter?"*
>
> *"What does dick mean?" comes a small innocent voice from the backseat.*
>
> *Oh shit, why did I forget our daughter and her younger, tiny impressionable ears?!*
>
> *"You see?" Dan said.*

I agreed to suck up my laughter and continued on with life as a mature responsible adult. We parked the car, got out, and

Andrew started walking all strange, hunched over, eyes darting around. Dan and I looked at him, puzzled.

> *He batted his gorgeous big blue eyes and said, "Well, I don't see any sperm coming from Dick's...I suppose it's safe to go in!"*
>
> *We both dissolved into a fit of giggles once again. Dan sighed, rolled his eyes and walked ahead of us with Chelsea. I regained my composure, took a deep breath and headed into the store where we were greeted by rows and rows of baskets with countless colors, sizes, and shapes of balls—balls of all sorts.*
>
> *Andrew and I instantly locked eyes and I read the sign. SALE on BALLS! "Dick's balls are on sale!"*

Thanks to the many supportive people in my life, I am slowly coming around to the idea that instilling this sense of humour in my son might make me a pretty great mom after all.

Take Regan anywhere that has a beach, sun, and a fancy cocktail. While there, she may show you the extra joint she has on two toes of each foot—she really IS one of a kind! Her boisterous laugh reverberates off the buildings in her townhouse complex, causing the parrot several houses over to mimic her. She's a karaoke queen who says the word "pickles" a lot, as a sneaky "replacement language" way to swear in class, or in the presence of her two children. Regan has been a passionate inclusive education teacher and advocate for over twenty years.

Janette

♥

You Can't Run With Us

"Is this how I'm going to die?" Anxiety danced between every shallow breath and bounced on my heart.

I had sweat in places I didn't even know you could sweat from. After too many convenient trips to McDonald's, I found myself out of shape and overweight, sitting on life's sideline.

When my husband's Instagram photos came across my feed, he was on a business trip enjoying a beer on a dock in Kelowna and I was in a bookstore in Regina having a panic attack over buying a twenty-dollar book. Our daughters were almost two and seven that summer and the three of us girls had taken a road trip to Saskatchewan to visit family, leaving my husband at home in BC to work.

One of our favourite things to do in Regina was to visit bookstores and browse with my sister-in-law. But the simple thought of buying myself a book caused a panic attack.

It takes a lot of practice ignoring one's self to be able to have a full-blown panic attack over buying a book. I had become a professional neglector; I had gotten really good at not treating myself to my own money.

Two years earlier, when I was pregnant with Zoe, I had decided that I was finally going to quit smoking for good. After fifteen years, I promised myself I was never going back. I sat in my doctor's office, unable to breathe, chest heaving, sweat pooling, heart racing; choking on my tears. I felt completely submerged underwater, the sound of the office muffled, certain I was having a heart attack. It turns out I'd been using cigarettes for years as a way to treat my undiagnosed anxiety.

Standing in the bookstore, amidst finding out my parents were separating, managing life with anxiety, two kids, being self-employed, and heavier than I'd ever been aside from when I was pregnant, I hated myself.

I had gotten good at hiding the truth that I was miserable. My sister-in-law had no idea that I was barely staying afloat.

After Ava's birth, I had experienced postpartum depression but truly didn't believe that I had with Zoe. However, when I look back, it just presented itself very differently for round two. Or maybe it was my parents splitting after thirty-seven years and feeling like everything I knew was a complete sham. If their marriage couldn't withstand their differences, how could mine? I mean, there was my husband drinking expensive beer on a dock and I couldn't justify a book.

*The Life Changing Magic Of Not Giving a F*ck* was the book that grabbed my attention and ultimately changed my life before I even opened it. I read the back, had a giggle, and thought to myself, how fitting. Nineteen dollars and ninety-five cents was the price of my sanity.

My chest heaved, I couldn't breathe, my heart pounded and I was back underwater but this time it was worse because I had a little audience watching me fall apart.

Standing in the aisle, scrolling my husband's Instagram, I found myself overwhelmed with anger. I made up all sorts of stories in my head about how much fun he was having, how he was happier without us, and it felt like he was broadcasting how good a time he was having to spite me.

With the twenty-dollar book still in hand, I sat quietly watching my girls thumb through the pages of various kids' books. I took a deep breath and the anger briefly cleared. I could see my husband in his true form: a loving, kind, hardworking man who wished no ill upon me or our children. My inner narrative was so used to saying bad things about myself that I had even begun making up false stories about my husband's behavior and even his intentions.

He was having a beer, there was no crime in that at all; my anxiety had taken over. I heard his voice say "buy the damn book" and realized that I was projecting my mother's current dislike for my father onto my own marriage. I had an unrealistic idea of what motherhood should be based on memories I had as a child of things I never wanted my children to experience.

Was he panicking over the price of the beer? Why was I so hung up on the price of a book? I realized that the story I was telling myself about the book and the twenty dollars, would eventually be the very same one my girls would tell themselves. If I didn't start showing them that I was worthy of love, respect, and time, they would think this was normal. If I didn't want my girls to ever live that way, why the hell was I okay living that way myself?

The next day, I drove back to the bookstore with the girls and bought myself that book!

Upon returning home to Vancouver, I dug out the Nike shoes I'd received as a gift years before and I set out on a mission to find some local mamas to run with. Moms are kind, gentle, patient, loving people; I'd be safe with them. I responded to a post on Facebook and walked to the community centre to meet them, a mixed bag of feelings—terrified, hopeful, sweaty, thirsty, and full of excuses. I took a deep breath and I said, "I'm a former smoker and I haven't run since I was like fifteen years old."

We set out on our run. Every time my feet hit the ground my brain throbbed. My lungs felt like they were collapsing. Everything hurt: my feet, my calves, my hips, my arms. I could feel the run pulsing through every single muscle. Why do people do this to themselves willingly?

I stopped to walk, and despite my protests, the other moms stopped and walked with me. No matter how many times I told them, "Keep going, I'll catch up," they insisted on staying with me. As I made my way back home after completing 3km in thirty-one minutes, I felt the pride I had craved my entire life. I hurt tremendously but I finally had a place that I fit into.

The next day, pain coursed through every single muscle. I hobbled sideways down the stairs to my basement to get the laundry, I vowed that by the next week I'd be able to keep up.

"I want to run faster than we did the other night," the main mom said. "We only get the chance to go out once a week so we want to make it as good of a workout as we can."

Then she offered to find me someone else to run with. I sat in that moment full of anger, embarrassment, sadness. I had never been in a running group before but this couldn't be what running groups were meant to be like. Instead of wallowing in sadness, I decided to run further, faster, and better than them.

Getting kicked out for being too slow ended up being one of the best things that ever happened to me. Just ten days after my first-ever run, I completed my first 5km run in 30:05.

January came around and my best friend challenged me to run the Vancouver Sun Run. Cockily I agreed, laughing, "Pfft...I got this." I didn't notice until after I paid that the Sun Run was 10km, not 5...CRAP!

My Dad had always said, "You're only as good as your word." So I posted my plan on social media hoping for some support. Through one of my followers, later turned friend, I became a sponsored runner to write for the Vancouver Sun blog. I would take the SportMedBC InTraining RunWalk program to reach 10km and start at the front of the line for the 2017 Vancouver SunRun.

I didn't know if I could handle getting kicked out of another group. I joined six weeks into their program and finally found one of the safest places I've ever felt. The other runners welcomed me openly, free of any shame, and with the loudest cheers I'd ever heard. "Janette!" Like a kindergarten child, I'd proudly place that sticker by my name week after week...I was doing it!

When things got hard they'd give me space to get mad at myself, to challenge myself to show up. When it got even harder, they'd loop back for me: I'd never be left behind. This was what a running group was supposed to be.

On the day of the race my best friend took off like a gazelle, long strides, full of power, she was there for a time goal. I was there for the experience. I cried the entire time. From the 10-year-old to the 65-year-old, and all the families lined up along the route cheering for every single runner.

For once there was no doubt and no shame. When I crossed that finish line with tear-stained cheeks and I saw my best friend cheering me on louder than the crowd itself, I felt incredibly proud...I had done it!

I have set and accomplished goals I never even knew I had. From countless 10Ks to two half marathons in 2020 and two full 42.2-km marathons in 2021, I learned that I am mentally stronger than I give myself credit for. When I tell myself I can't run anymore, I can quickly identify that "I can't" and "I don't want to" are two different things.

The irony is not lost on me that this story is going live in a twenty-dollar book. I'm a firm believer in full-circle moments—over the years I've had plenty—but this one feels like two halves of a puzzle clicking perfectly together.

Not long ago, I was a traumatized young woman riddled with anxiety, needing the approval to buy a twenty-dollar book, kicked out of the running group for being too slow, dying to feel like I was good enough. And now here I am, a mother of two thriving children, happily married, a marathon runner, and running my own running clinic.

I wish I could tell you that the anxiety is gone but it's something I manage daily, and running helps. I am the best version of myself after I complete a run. I schedule my runs like I do my kids' activities; I don't ask for the time, I take it.

Running is my time to mentally clean my room. I take inventory of what's bothering me/sitting on my shoulders and during my long runs, I put those things away.

Would I ever want my girls to ignore their own needs, speak negatively to themselves, or give up because someone said they weren't good enough? Hell no!! So my "darlings", Ava and Zoe, here I am telling you you're worth it. If you ever doubt how deserving and loved you are, "just buy the damn book!" I promise you won't regret it!

This mom of two has always wanted to go to Rome but right now she'd settle for anywhere all-inclusive with lots of naps. Nothing keeps her up at night: Janette sleeps "like a husband." As the Online Communications Manager for SportMedBC, the company she originally started running through, she's managed to turn her passion for running into a job. Though it sounds cliché, running has honestly saved her these past five years.

@AVATOZOE

here's your
PERMISSION SLIP:

to DANCE
to take a YOGA CLASS
to MAKE *a* BIG SPLASH
to TAKE *a* DETOUR
to STAY *in your* LANE
to BE BRAVE

Jennifer

Bonus Mom

By the age of six, I knew I never wanted kids. Motherhood only led to self-destruction. After all, I had spent my childhood observing abusive partnerships, addiction as a method of coping, and believing that nothing is what it seems.

So when faced with a crumbling marriage and a positive pregnancy test, panic was truly the only reasonable reaction.

It wasn't until after Brayden was born that I forced myself to face the fact that it was time to leave his father. Denial is a very easy state of mind to stay in when it only affects you, but now I had this little human whose entire well-being was in my hands. My biggest concern became making sure my son was okay no matter the cost—even if leaving meant I was about to fight a war I was not prepared for.

Ignorantly, I had not truly considered the depths of vindictiveness that were yet to come and I became terrified that this one decision was going to be the death of us both. I started to lose control, and if not for the intimate circle of people keeping me grounded, I am not sure I would have come out the other side. There were nights of no sleep, wondering what was next, drive-bys, threats, wildly false accusations to children's aid, financial devastation and an all-out war on how we could co-parent. At one point even exchanges at the police station became hostile and aggressive. I believe he felt untouchable, because no matter how brash the behaviour, no real repercussions followed. Restraining orders were broken, assault charges thrown out and there was a complete lack of concern for how this was impacting his son. I endured five years of living in fear of what was to come. Each day more volatile than the previous one; there was no restraining order in the world that brought me peace of mind. I would not gain any clarity or feeling of power back until much later in life, after losing what felt like every sense of self along the way.

During some of those darkest moments I was able to come to terms with my own childhood—growing up around alcoholism made more of an impact on my identity than even I was quite ready to face. These times of reflection gave me the ability to gain a new understanding of how easy it is to hit rock bottom when you're in a toxic situation. Possibly some of these misguided illusions, was just my mother shielding her daughter from pain, like I now was doing for my very own child. To say the least, motherhood, for me, had become everything my childhood self had come to expect: painful, self-limiting, and dangerous.

I did eventually find my inner light again and remarried. Marc was my teenage sweetheart, one of the first men who ever captivated me. As fate tends to work we lived our separate lives, maintaining contact over the years, knowing deep down we would eventually end up where we always belonged. Had we not walked our separate paths our future wouldn't have come together the way it did.

Ten years later our partnership was going to look a lot different: our previous relationships had brought children into the equation. In an instant I had two boys the exact same age, two years old, like twins who are not biologically related. One that called me mom and one that called me Jenny. Each child brought completely different personality traits: Brayden was outgoing and funny while DJ was quiet and observant. Becoming a compatible family was a steep learning curve. Our children's differences, involvement of our exes, court dates, and downright maliciousness from the outside brought many challenges, but we persevered. I felt being a mother was already hard enough, but step-parenting without pregnancy, infancy, and bonding, was a hurdle. I needed to learn how to navigate the highly charged emotions that came with this new dynamic.

I wasn't prepared for all the opinions and judgements of being a step-parent. I can not tell you how many times DJ referred to me as Jen in public, almost always creating an uncomfortable pause with our audience and then an unprovoked explanation that I am not his real mom. Parent-teacher meetings, doctor's appointments, it never failed. There were times I wanted to defend my title to complete strangers based on a single word.

It's unnerving how much merit is put on the word *mother.* Was I less of a role model or parental figure because I wasn't called Mom? Surely there were other stepmothers as the primary caregivers. Why did society make this feel so foreign for stepmothers while praising stepfathers?

I have learned to handle the spirited sense of home that has become for us, sharing holidays, uncomfortable conversations, and unique love and bonds.

There have been moments as a woman and a mom I am incredibly proud of and others...not so much. If asked what the most challenging aspect of my parental journey is, I'd have to say loving a child like he is my own while navigating the reality that this love is nothing like anything I have experienced. Only those privileged enough to earn it will understand the sentiment behind these words.

As a grown woman raising a blended family I have gained a new appreciation for my stepfather. My dad was the living example that blood doesn't make bonds, the people that show up do. He modelled to me that choosing to love someone without being obligated to love them is a powerful gift. He taught me what unconditional love is, supporting my mother while she mended from her past, while loving her daughter as if I was his own. His presence was a living testament that although parenting is hard, marriage is hard, hell life is hard, you don't give up on the ones you cherish the most. Raising a blended family of my own I now truly understand how much of a father he really was. I only hope one day DJ reflects on his relationship with me with half as much admiration as I have for my dad.

Our home has become a crazy mixture of three boys, Marc and I welcomed another son, Morgan in 2013. Each of their needs are unique, their struggles individual, and what they require from me, as a mother, varies widely.

Brayden has grown into the kindest, most loving soul. Although he continues to deal with emotional abuse from his father he strives to be the exact opposite and shows everyone what good truly looks like. He works hard to meet his goals and has never let his past define him. He will never truly understand how proud I am to be his mother, he alone singlehandedly made me want more from life and shows me how to be the best I can be.

DJ is naturally brilliant, hard-working, a give-you-the-shirt-off-his-back type of kid. He makes me smile daily but may also contribute to some of the yelling in the house, I mean he is a teenager now and the big brown eyes and cute curly hair have been replaced with a husky voice and six-foot-tall presence. I have watched him struggle to see where he feels he belongs, and what family means to him. He is still finding his footing but I have no doubt he will always walk the right path, because he is pure and genuine and I believe his goodness will always shine through. Although he did not meet demons like Brayden, he has his own insecurities that he will learn to accept with time and age.

Morgan is the smartest, most thoughtful young man, and I am so proud of his resilience. I know he will achieve whatever he sets out to do in life, maybe more cautiously than most, but the result will be the same: spectacular. He is an old soul with a child's perspective and wisdom unlike anything I have ever seen.

Morgan, like his father, was diagnosed with Tourette's. I have the unique perspective of watching Tourette's consume two people I love very much, a disorder that bonds them indefinitely. Being a young child/grown man with comorbidities like severe anxiety doesn't often make sense to outsiders, or even to themselves. Throw a pandemic into the mix and you can imagine the uncertainty and fear that manifested. Covid life in our household has been challenging and scary with an extra sense of precautions.

When I am alone and reflecting I feel that emotionally maybe this is all too draining. Am I selfish for even saying I'm mentally exhausted? Who am I to complain when the people I love have so much to deal with, I am supposed to be the glue that holds us together. I never imagined parenting two teenagers, and a young man with an adult thought process on a good day never mind in the middle of a pandemic. Nor did I fathom we would still be dealing with verbal abuse from Brayden's father twelve years later. Although my heart aches for my son I have learned to set aside these feelings and do what is right by him. Brayden one day will reach his own conclusions, and that is all I can ask. It has become a fine balance of their happiness and mine but this is our life and I wouldn't change it for anything.

I myself am learning how to put my insecurities in check, how to grow as a parent, and a person, to stop seeking validation from strangers. Part of this process is learning how to be a successful co-parent. With DJ, comes the very important woman he calls Mom and it's my job to be supportive, kind, and care about their relationship just as much as I care about ours. His mother and I have developed a bond that is centred around the well-being of DJ. She and I collaborate about exchanges, important events, and just life in general. We have open discussions, occasional dinners together, trips to amusement parks, soccer games. Personal growth comes in many forms and making sure my kids know I would do anything in the world to show them they are loved by many, is one of them.

I am trying to give my boys a better childhood than the one I experienced, however I haven't a clue what a good parent actually is. Motherhood (birth or bonus) does not come with instructions, there is no right or wrong way and it looks different for every situation. I want my mom to know how incredibly proud I am of her, her path was harder than most but she made it to the other side—and I love you! If there is one thing I wish for my kids to remember, it is that I love them more than peanut butter loves jelly and always tried to be the best I knew how to be, even though that was far from picture perfect. Motherhood has shown me that you can overcome hard things, and you do get a second chance at making life right. With every bit of pain there have been a thousand smiles, for every mistake made, a thousand steps forward and for every tear shed, a million laughs. Maybe when they are parents they can take lessons learned from us and do better but most of all I hope they appreciate every step of the journey that shaped them into the amazing young men they are.

On a lazy day,* Grey's Anatomy *and take-out pizza make for a pretty happy Jennifer. She loves her three boys, 'obviously,' never-ending cups of tea, and there's a special place in her heart and on her playlists for Tom Petty. Jennifer's strong public speaking skills have helped her along the way during her successful career in the world of veterinary sales. She loves horseback riding and dreams of one day traveling to Peru to see the rainforest.

All Aboard

My husband stood above me as I lay there, belly open, life given but no sound. His tears landed on my face.

Alarms sounded. Controlled chaos filled the room.

Silence.

No cry, no sound.

I wouldn't hear that little voice until three years later.

Eleven minutes. How could anyone survive without oxygen for eleven minutes? But my son did. I felt trapped, like watching someone under ice, seeing them struggle to find the opening to the surface, and I could do nothing to help. With panic starting to ensue, my husband and I's hands squeezed a little tighter, as we too, held our breath; hoping, anticipating and trusting our son would find the surface. A mucus blockage was finally released and he gasped and gulped all the air he could.

"Babe, we have a son."

"Go with him, follow him, wherever they take him, you go." I whispered this, as I winced from the pain I was starting to feel, as my epidural began to fade. I let go of my husband's hand, he kissed my lips and was ushered to be with our son.

The complications of my C-section were real, and what should have been a routine surgery was narrowly dismissed as a near-death experience for both my son and I.

"Carolyn, our son's life was saved by a South African doctor, the procedure he performed is not normally used here in Canada. Without him, we would not have our son."

"I guess, it's our lucky day then!"

"Babe, I think it was more than lucky!"

"Yes, but remember what I said two days ago?"

Two days prior when my water broke, I had said that our baby would be born on August 22nd, since it was all our lucky numbers. I was actually due in September, but August is the eighth month, my lucky number is eight, and two is my husband's; it just made sense.

We would learn later on that I had undiagnosed preeclampsia. During my C-section the doctors could not stop me from bleeding. I had two pumps inserted into my abdomen to pump the excess blood out, but it would not be enough. Five days later, infection spread, and my abdomen could no longer withstand the pressure. The incision that gave birth to my son burst open, staples not strong enough to grip, and I collapsed on the hospital floor.

"Hi Mom! Hi Dad!" His eyes look at his little hand waving as he swooshes past us like a freight train thundering down the tracks. His wheels go click, and his wheels go clack. My son only has one speed, full steam. He runs on his tiptoes everywhere he goes, always so careful to never miss a step.

We would miss a few steps in our first six months together. I lost my dad to cancer, Reece had to have an unexpected surgery and I developed a heart condition that was linked to my pregnancy. What seems like a casual grocery list of items now, brought a lot of pain, grief, and anger that I fought so hard to not let crumble me. We tried our hardest to stay the course and for the most part we did. My son was reaching milestones and I began to feel the true joy that motherhood brings to one's soul.

It's not often you get the chance to flirt with death. Never once did I think when I would go to deliver my child that so quickly the life we had made could potentially be taken away, as well as my own. You can't prepare for it, no prenatal class will cover it, but we lived it.

We lived.

We had fallen through cracks, I had been misdiagnosed, and we had been overlooked. I was downright petrified. I had no idea how this birth trauma would affect our son, how we would all recover, and what lay ahead of us.

Lying in my hospital bed that night, alone and exhausted from days of labour and major surgery, I listened as intently as I could. My son and husband had been airlifted to a larger hospital and the doctor's last words were, "I want you to know that I tried my best."

I knew, in that moment, I had to promise myself to always try my best. Whatever curves we would encounter, or hills we would have to climb, I knew if I tried my best, it would be enough.

Until it wasn't.

Three years later I felt the eyes of other parents, their judgements and all of their half-hearted, "Oh you know boys just develop a little slower." The laughs, the stares and the "boys are crazy," comments.

I watched the hitting, crying, and destructive behaviours and then received unsolicited advice from other parents. The struggle to understand his actions, and hearing their words wore me down and bruised my heart. And still, I couldn't understand my son.

Those moments of complete dysregulation would transport me back to the days after his birth when I would grip the hall railing and lean hard into the wall to keep myself upright, as I would make my way slowly down the excruciatingly long corridor to eventually arrive at the NICU doors, too weak to actually open them. I would peer through and wait, smile and wait again for a nurse to come with the wheelchair. At any point my knees could give way.

I would stare through more glass, trying to memorize every one of his little features. My heart would ache as I watched the nurses care for him, as I observed from my wheelchair, too weak to care for my son.

He carefully lays each piece of track, perfectly placing each of his trains, connecting their magnets with a click. Pushing them forward and back, his tummy flat on the ground, so they are at eye level, focusing, and memorizing every detail of every train.

"Where are you on the ASD Waitlist?"

"Pardon?"

"ASD...Autism..."

"I am aware of what ASD stands for...and, well, we aren't on any waitlist because I had no idea my son has autism!"

"Well, the behaviours I see here today are not typical, you need to connect with your doctor and get on a list."

After Reece's two-year-old check-up, we were sent to a specialist appointment to see if or maybe why he snored. The conversation sent me into a tailspin and ultimately changed our family's lives. I was completely shaken and caught off guard. I remember saying, "OK I will look into it, thank you," and walking out. I buckled my son into his car seat, walked around to my door and got in. I sat there. I turned back to look at him.

I said his name, "Reece."

He did not make eye contact with me.

I said his name again. In fact, I yelled it, "Reece honey," I waited.

He never looked, he didn't even acknowledge I was there.

Tears welled and flooded over.

At that moment, I knew.

My best wasn't enough.

I encountered a humbling realization, and the weight of those thoughts paralyzed me. I had always felt I had been a champion for my son. We had survived a lot in our three short years together and I always prided myself on being the absolute best mom I could be to him.

But here is *the* difference. Doing my best, and being enough are two different things.

I am not a speech pathologist, a behaviour consultant, physiotherapist, or occupational therapist. My son needs all of these people. I cannot provide what they provide. I am simply his mom.

With any diagnosis comes grief. I thought back to all the traditional "milestones," or "benchmarks," I had read about in my baby books, and had so carefully monitored for the last three years. I wanted to tear every page in those books. I began to question my own self, my abilities of a mother and grieve my own lack of awareness. How could I have not seen any of these signs?

What I didn't expect to grieve were the everyday moments that seem routine, easy, non-issues that aren't. Making friends, family photos, eating at restaurants, or going to new places. I found myself questioning everything. Did I prep him enough, did I pack his apple and little zippered pouch full of his trains, had I made the right decision switching daycares, and created the best team? I don't know, but I feel it all. I feel completely overwhelmed. Every night I look at the stack of books I was advised to read and think about the ideas, theories, and practices I was supposed to try to implement and it's really hard to know my best isn't enough.

This summer Reece was diagnosed with autism, and despite all my feelings of guilt, defeat, and anxiety there is an overwhelming sense of clarity. My son has autism and that doesn't change him, in fact, the only thing it changes is our perspective. It provides his dad and me, the rest of our family, and his care team, much more insight into how Reece thinks, perceives, feels and learns in this world. The autism diagnosis helped me see my son clearly for the very first time. Like staring through the glass in the NICU all over again.

When the steam lifts and you see the engine, you see all its beauty. Standing tall, bravely starting to inch its wheels forward, proud of its paintwork and ready to set off down the tracks, knowing that his track is so clearly his own. He may not be the strongest but he'll get there in good time, on his schedule: he'll stop at every station along his route, he'll pick up and drop off passengers, greeting them and making sure they're safe and comfortable. He will wave to onlookers, and he'll never be afraid to blow his whistle if he encounters danger. Pistons continue to fire, as he is so sure of his strength and abilities, that there is never any doubt he will bravely pass through every dark tunnel and cross every bridge.

I finally hear his distinctive little voice, "All aboard, Mommy, all aboard..."

♥

Carolyn is passionate about teaching—she's the coolest teacher in town....jk! As half of the two-sister MomBabe duo, it's no surprise Carolyn's bookshelf is full of memoirs. Her dreams take her away to Italy, with all the espresso, and all the pasta (OK, and pizza!) Thinking about ALL THE THINGS keeps her late-night wheels spinning while her family, coffee, and long summer days make all the thinking worthwhile. She appreciates a well-curated home with a good '90s playlist on repeat.

Christina

Wishbone

I had always dreamt of my wedding: the dress, the ring, the flowers, and walking down the aisle with my dad toward that special person. But there was another special person I didn't think about—my mother-in-law.

The first time I met my future mother-in-law was long before my husband and I had started dating. Peter and I were just friends— two twenty-somethings with little responsibility and big aspirations. I would describe Peter as the quintessential "nice guy," you know the one. The one who you know would never ask you so you have to build the courage to ask him out after dating all the "not-so-nice" guys who break your heart over and over. I always wondered why Peter never had a girlfriend until I met his mom, Nancy. She came off the same way she drank her rum and Cokes. Strong.

Nancy was a powerful mix of Doris Roberts from *Everybody Loves Raymond*, with her passive-aggressive tone and love for her son who could do no wrong; and Robert DeNiro from *Meet the Fockers*, where I wasn't sure if I was ever going to break the barrier into the "circle of trust." She always wore shorts, runners, and packed a Velcro wallet. She didn't carry a purse. She never wore makeup, and I think used Vaseline as skin cream.

I was the first girlfriend Peter ever introduced to his mom and dad. It was his dad's 70th birthday party and I met his parents and all of their closest friends on the same night. Forty years of friendships filled the backyard. We had been friends for six years but now I was walking in as "the girlfriend." Big city girl meets a small-town boy. I wanted to make a strong first impression, so I brought flowers and wine, only to be given the backhanded compliment "Oh! pink flowers. I don't like anything pink." It felt like taking on a pack of wolves all at once. In hindsight there was only one lone wolf I had to keep an eye on. At the end of the evening, believing I was welcomed with open arms, I hugged Nancy goodbye.. This would be the last hug I'd receive for eleven years.

Nancy didn't make it easy to love her. When I showed up I was never sure who I was going to get. Friendly, ready to chat, or not letting me in the door when I popped over. I can't pinpoint exactly when our relationship shifted to her not speaking to me. I would try small subtle gestures like bringing a new hanging basket for her back deck. Always pink. Yes, two can play this game.

My husband loves his mom and yes, he could be described as the typical "mama's boy" but he always backed me. When she would call the house (it was 2009 so we still had a landline and call display) and I would answer, "Hi Nanc." Click. She would hang up on me. Every time. "Your Mom called," I'd say. Peter would respond with "She can call back. You live here too." He always gave me the confidence to never doubt his love for me. Peter told me countless times, "Christina, I'm marrying you, not her."

We were engaged for a year and as much as I wanted to involve Nancy in the planning and all the pre-wedding celebrations she would always decline or no-show. She didn't RSVP, show up to the rehearsal dinner, or come for family photos. But she did attend our wedding. In true Nancy fashion she wore flip flops and a Hawaiian shirt, with cargo shorts. Two hundred guests and only one person in shorts.

She always carried a gold digital camera, it fit easily into a cargo pocket. The mother-of-the-groom took photos the whole ceremony. We'd paid thousands for a professional photographer and there she was clicking away in the front row.

Nancy came up to me after the ceremony. I was draped in a a long white lace dress and she was wearing a loud floral print.

With two rum and Cokes in hand, she offered me her drink of choice.

"Shall we make a toast, Mrs. Walsh?"

"Suuuuuuure." Holding my breath.

"Welcome to the family."

No hug, but I knew she meant it.

After the wedding, Nancy and I took some baby steps forward. She still didn't make it easy but she no longer hung up when I called and I was allowed to come into her house again.

She was protective and scared; I believe she was afraid of change. Letting go as a mother is the most difficult part of parenting. Being a stay-at-home mother was her identity. If she wasn't taking care of someone who was she? Her son had lived at home into his twenties and I believe she felt a deep sense of loss. I realized later on that it wouldn't have mattered who the woman was: Nancy's rude and frankly bizarre behavior wasn't about me, it was about losing her son.

On our first Thanksgiving after the wedding, Nancy suggested we invite my parents to dinner as well. I had no idea how to cook a turkey but my parents agreed to come early to deal with the bird and I'd prepare the rest. While I was setting the table that afternoon, I got a call from my parents—there had been an accident on the highway and they would be delayed a few hours.

I called my husband.

"Christina, you do have one option..."

"What? Order Chinese food?"

"Okay, two options. But you could call my Mom and ask her to help you."

With a deep sigh, I nodded, pursed my lips and mumbled, "Fine."

Nancy showed up about twenty minutes later with a Walmart bag in hand, wearing shorts. Obviously.

She taught me how to stuff the bird and said it was best to cook the turkey upside down so all juices run into the breast and the meat doesn't dry out. I've been cooking my turkey like this ever since. But what she was best at was carving the turkey. She was meticulous, like a surgeon with a scalpel. That old bird sliced a bird like no other west of the Rocky Mountains. I had never seen anyone carve a turkey the way she did, and she always found the wishbone with laser-beam accuracy. I would stand there in awe, watching her with impeccable focus. She would then confidently pull the wishbone and tuck it on the window sill so it would dry, allowing us to make a wish at Christmas.

Inside the Walmart bag was an electric knife she had bought me so that I could learn how to carve a turkey. I still have the electric knife. She also bought me an iron—I don't use that.

Over the years, Nancy and I had many ups and downs, I tried really hard to involve her in special ways. When I was pregnant with our first baby I invited her to come to my ultrasound. That's right, I left my husband and my mom and took her. She would be the first person to meet our baby.

I used to always say she loves her son and she loves her grandchildren, and that's all that matters. She doesn't have to love me. I had the love I needed from the people I needed it from. I didn't want to have to convince someone to love me.

When our daughter was born we began noticing small signs of Nancy's forgetfulness. On the second day home from the hospital, she told us she would never be able to take care of our daughter, she didn't feel comfortable babysitting. I took this as another sign that she didn't love me. But, she wasn't trying to hurt me, this was the only way she knew to keep her granddaughter safe.

The diagnosis was frontotemporal dementia. She was sixty-three.

When our daughter was eighteen months old, I was back to work after maternity leave, trying to balance daycare, a two hour commute, and Peter being on night shift. I wasn't able to get home in time for my husband to make it to work—we just needed someone to watch our daughter for about fifteen minutes a day. Nancy seemed like the only option. She had said she would never babysit or change a diaper but she agreed to the fifteen minutes. One afternoon, after relieving her from her brief child-minding shift, I asked Nancy if she wanted to host a BBQ for my father-in-law's birthday.

"What? He has a birthday coming up?"

"Mhm, it's in a few weeks."

"When's his birthday?"

I still thought she was joking around. "June 5, his birthday is a Friday."

She grabbed a piece of paper and wrote down 'June 5—Bob's birthday.'

Two weeks later at the BBQ, everyone brought potato salad. Six bowls of potato salad laid out on the table. Nancy had told everyone to bring the same thing. That's when I knew. I also knew we weren't leaving our daughter with her even for a few minutes.

Losing her keys and forgetting to turn off the stove accelerated into a more significant cognitive decline, often leaving her agitated and irritated. Slowly she began finding difficulty with words—repetitive with questions and stories. Her mind deteriorating. We were losing a parent. I watched her do puzzles on the floor with my daughter and saw her struggle to put them together. Simple tasks became easier for my three-year-old but impossible for her sixty-three-year-old grandmother.

"You're such a smart girl," She would say, over and over and over.

Our circle was small and people began to notice. Nancy had a few close friends who had accepted her for forty years so they were right by her side for daily walks and repetitive talks, and always picked up her calls even when she had already spoken with them that day. Acceptance was hard for everyone. Grieving the loss of someone while they are right in front of you carries painful anticipatory grief. Waiting, watching. Little deaths everyday.

When the time came to move Nancy to a long-term care facility the tokens she received from her best friend were photos. A beautifully labelled album filled with pictures of all of the people who loved her. This gesture reminded me that in the end, the best heirlooms are the photographs. The little gold camera she had carried in her cargo pocket was how she remembered her day—we found thousands of pictures downloaded to her laptop. Shots of what most would describe as 'nothing' but when Nancy spent long hours sitting at her desk, she was scrolling the photos.

My daughters will not ask for the fine china or the sports memorabilia that hangs in the office. The treasures are the photographs because these will be the reminders of a life well-lived. I also want to write the stories before it's too late. While I can still remember them.

I want our children to know my relationship with their grandmother wasn't perfect, far from it. But we tried. That no matter how many times she closed the door or hung up, I kept showing up. I loved her because she loved my husband and my children with all of her being. I know this now, as a mother myself.

A terrible disease took my children's grandma from them. It took her memory, but I'll be damned if I will let it take ours. When Nancy didn't know who we were, she knew we were her family. She recognized me as the "mother figure." We would still call her Mom and she would look at me and say, "I'm not a Mom." She no longer recognized herself in the role she had fought me so hard to keep. One of the last things Nancy said to me was, "You're a nice mother to them. You must love them."

Over the years many people have told me, "She talks the world of you." I would schluff them off and roll my eyes. "Really? She's never said that to me." But deep down in my heart I knew.

I remember saying goodbye to her the night before we took her to the long-term care facility. I wish I'd hugged her a little tighter. I wish I'd whispered, "Thank you for loving us all so goddamn fiercely. For teaching us to fight, to not care what other people think, and that beating your own drum sometimes makes the most sense."

But what can I do when my daughters' grandmother can't tell her side of the story? I can make sure to write the love letter. Because my darling daughters' grandmother loved them both. Both of them were her world. Nothing mattered more. She just never got the chance to tell them.

And for me, it's forgiveness. Giving her grace because she was losing more than a son, she was losing herself in the process. How terrifying that must have felt. So I set the judgement and resentment aside and wrap myself up in the good, in that one last hug, because in the end I know that time, death, or a bad memory can't take away the love.

And every Thanksgiving when I pull out my electric knife to carve the upside-down turkey, my daughters standing at the kitchen counter, we laugh as we try to find the goddamn wishbone. No luck—yet—we'll keep wishing.

♥

As class president in grade school and voted "rage against the system" in high school, Christina was destined for a life in politics. You can often find a Domino's Pizza box in her fridge, anything country on her playlist, and a decaf americano in her hand. Christina is an optimist who never finishes a drink which means her glass is always half full ;) Do not burp in her presence, it totally grosses her out. Her favourite book is this one, duh.

here's your
PERMISSION SLIP:

to LIVE *your* LEGACY
to BE *in the* PHOTO
to WRITE *the* STORY
to SHARE *your* SECRETS
to be EXACTLY *who you* WANT *to be*
to KNOW *you are* LOVED

Ashley

♥

I Just Kept Holding

The instability, unpredictability, and lack of control were what really rocked me. I didn't factor in that this might not work for me; that my motherhood journey could end at any moment. With every visit to the fertility clinic, the doctor could tell me, "It's over." Each day of injections, each blood test, each ultrasound, each procedure, let alone once pregnancy actually started. If it ever started.

I thought stabbing myself with needles would be the hard part. Or maybe the out-of-control emotions I was told might bombard me while I filled my body with fertility hormones. It was shocking to realize the needles and crazy drugs were the easy part. At least they were predictable.

I knew what drugs to take, what time to take them, how much of each medication to mix, and how to inject the concoction into the fat of my stomach. After a day or so, I learned how one of the drugs left a throbbing pain at the injection site and another one burned for a few seconds as it plunged in. After a few more days, I knew that I could keep my emotions in check. I was hyper-aware of my feelings but I could control them. I wasn't crying hysterically or yelling at my husband like the nurse said might happen. I was okay.

I didn't realize how bruised my stomach would become, how it would be dotted with yellow, purple, and black. I didn't account for the fact that my stomach would swell so much I looked pregnant. That I would have to wear my "fat pants" to work to try and hide it.

I remember sitting in the changing room at the fertility clinic, a thin paper sheet wrapped around my waist, waiting for my final ultrasound after twelve days of hormone injections. Through the wall, I could hear the muffled conversation between the doctor and nurse, "I know, I feel so bad for her, she's only thirty-one, there is just a small chance..." Tears filled my eyes and a massive lump formed in my throat. Tension crept up my back, over my shoulders, and into my chest as I struggled to keep my breathing steady.

What did I do wrong? Did I do an injection ten minutes too late? It took me an hour to drive home from the clinic, was that too long to get my meds into the fridge?

With a heavy breath, I walked into the exam room, sat in the chair next to my husband, and tried not to let the tears spill as the doctor looked at me with sad, kind eyes. My husband squeezed my hand but I couldn't look at him. She explained that there was a small chance the procedure could work. If we moved forward with the egg retrieval, I was likely looking at one egg. One. Egg.

It seemed like an obvious choice, keep going, but this egg retrieval was a $10,000 decision. We either quit now and try again to get more eggs, or we take a huge risk and move forward for a cool 10K. My doctor left us with this..."It only takes one." One tiny miracle.

Talk about a mind spiral. What if this one was THE one? What if this was a huge waste of time, money, and emotional effort? My husband and I went through the stereotypical pros and cons list as we counted down the few hours until we had to make a decision.

"I'm not sure we should do this," I said, "It's probably not going to work, maybe we should just start over."

"What if we do it again and end up in the exact same situation?" he said.

Well, shit. We had to take a chance.

I raced to the clinic to pick up my trigger shots which would cause my body to ovulate my hopeful little egg. I had to inject them at precisely the right time. At 11 p.m. that night, the pinch of the needle and the burn of the drugs spread over my stomach like a coloured bath bomb dropping into the tub.

I said a little *wish*, please, and hoped the universe would hear me.

We did it. We had one egg.

One viable egg.

The next day we found out our brave little egg, our long shot, had successfully fertilized.

Holy shit.

It kept growing. Multiplying cells. Doing exactly what it was supposed to do.

Day two.

Day three.

Yes.

I held my breath.

We set the date for the embryo transfer.

Day four.

Day five—transfer day, Baby.

That beautiful little blastocyst was placed directly into my uterus. Now I had to wait two weeks to find out if I was pregnant.

Wait...what?

Two weeks...just waiting...

The clinic very strictly advises against taking any preliminary pregnancy tests. So, of course, I didn't wait two weeks, because duh, I could take a pregnancy test at home. And cross my fingers. And toes. And hope.

So, on day ten, I crept into our bathroom.

Positive.

I told myself to shut up and remain calm and definitely keep this secret from my husband who, I mean, should have known I would obviously do this, but somehow didn't.

I could get my own hopes up but couldn't handle the extra weight of anyone else's.

For the next four days, positive.

On day fourteen, I went for my blood test with cautious optimism. Later that day I received a call.

I was officially pregnant.

Cue tears, snot, and all the ugly crying. I told my husband but kept my home pregnancy testing to myself. Our bodies shook as we embraced tightly, filled with incredulous happiness, tears, and laughter. (I eventually told him about my secret tests and he responded with a wide eyed, "Ashley!!!" then rolled his eyes and put his hand to his head, "I should have known you would do that." See, told you).

I carried our baby for the next eight or so months and after a thirty-six-plus-hour labour (three hours of pushing, people) and an emergency C-section (I mean, why not at this point), delivered a beautiful, healthy baby girl.

Our sweet Madelyn.

When Madelyn turned one, in the hope of having a second child, we started another cycle of IVF. This time, I knew what to expect. I felt prepared.

Again, with only one harvested egg, by some miracle, I became pregnant. Amazing!

A few weeks later, I woke up feeling...nothing. The nausea, the tiredness...were all gone. A new kind of sickness hit me and I knew.

We went to the fertility clinic later that week. I will never forget the doctor's words.

"No heartbeat."

She told me that this had happened to her.

"It will hurt," she said, "physically and emotionally."

She was right.

I lost our baby. My baby.

The clinic gave me a "kit" of supplies so I could send tissues to the lab to be checked for defects. Information that might help if we tried again. It could also tell us if we had lost our son or our daughter.

I had to know.

A week or so after my miscarriage nothing had happened. Physically. I could keep waiting or I could take some medication to help my body along. I opted for the meds.

What followed was probably the worst experience of my life.

I tasted salt from the tears running into my mouth. Crouching over the toilet, with my "kit", wearing rubber gloves, I fished through the blood and tissue in the bowl, trying to find what may have been my baby so I could put him or her into a urine collection container.

I went into a local lab, the container in my pocket holding what I believed was my baby.

I've never experienced that type of grief. Everything was so heavy and moved so slowly. The sting of a fresh wound on my heart as I handed the container over.

Some wounds will never heal.

Two days later, I departed to Ontario for my first work trip after being back from maternity leave.

Yep.

I could have cancelled the trip but I didn't want to tell anyone why. Not because I was embarrassed or ashamed. It was just too fresh. Too painful. Too raw. I couldn't even think about the miscarriage without crying. The thought of actually telling someone what had happened seemed worse than going on the trip.

So I left with my laptop bag stuffed full of enormous pads. I needed eight bathroom trips to get throughout each day. Click, click, click, down the marble hall, past the people.

Squish, squish, squish, the pads continued to fill with blood and my heart continued to break.

A few months later, I was ready to try it again. We went ahead with the bruised-banana-belly procedure and retrieved five eggs. FIVE! Wow! But by day three, only one of the eggs was looking okay.

We were optimistic; we knew it only takes one.

On day five, a voicemail from the lab tech asked me to call for my update. His voice cracked in the message. With a deep breath, I called back and he confirmed..."They stopped growing. You don't have anything to transfer. This cycle is over."

We were crushed. Deflated like a sad, old birthday balloon. All of the emotional energy, physical discomfort, mental stress, and financial stretch...for nothing.

My husband and I spent a long time talking, debating, researching. We decided to try one more time. One last, final, attempt.

We got two eggs. By day five, I had the one and only blastocyst remaining transferred into my uterus.

I held my breath.

I kept holding it while we waited for two weeks to find out if I was pregnant. Once more when the clinic confirmed I was pregnant. And again, when we heard the heartbeat for the first time.

I just kept holding.

A few weeks later, I got up to use the bathroom in the middle of the night. I pulled down my pj bottoms and sat on the toilet. Something felt strange...I stood up and blood rushed down my legs. The toilet bowl was red.

No, no, no.

I woke my husband and cried. I called the emergency line at the clinic and booked an ultrasound for later that morning.

Anxiety and panic washed over me. I could barely breathe. I braced myself.

The doctor started the ultrasound, looked at me, and smiled.

"Listen," she said, as she turned up the volume. A beautiful healthy heartbeat filled the room.

At thirty-nine weeks, we welcomed our smiley Sadie baby into the world.

All of it, everything, was worth it for our girls. My girls. I love them fiercely.

They are so young yet already so full of life and fire. Their sparkling bright light reminds me every day to go after what you want. Try. Try again. Failure and the unknown can be scary...but there just might be something beautiful on the other side of that fear. That, I want them to know.

It only takes one miracle to change a life. I was lucky enough to get two.

Ashley lives that corporate life and dreams of a family trip to Maui where the fam can spend the days beachside playing in the water and sneaking a few cocktails! In reality, on rainy Sundays while the kids sleep, you might find her cozied up on the couch with a hot coffee or glass of wine, fuzzy blanket, and a binge list of the latest on Netflix. She also loves a good Hallmark Christmas movie and is a surprisingly good cart-wheeler. If you're a slow walker, don't get in her way.

Jenn

♥

Unexpected

My dad wasn't supposed to die at age sixty-two. He had plans to spend his retirement hosting family BBQs, hiking in Palm Springs, biking in Italy, and finding inspiration in the local mountains for his oil paintings. He'd budgeted enough money to live a full life until he was ninety-one. He would have loved seeing his family grow and been an incredible grandpa.

On Valentine's Day, I was recovering from being dumped a few months earlier. For the first time ever, I'd called in sick to work without actually being sick. I was at home feeling sorry for myself in a puddle of self-pity, jelly beans, and reality TV. I was twenty-nine years old.

A call from my mum interrupted my wallowing. Dad had fallen while playing tennis and she asked if I could meet her. I was annoyed that my indulgence had been interrupted, but my parents weren't the type to ask needlessly for support. I got in my hand-me-down Volvo, turned up Taylor Swift's *Red* album—my breakup soundtrack—and headed for the tennis club where my family were longtime members.

While I drove, I brainstormed that if my Dad had broken a leg we could convert their downstairs room so he wouldn't have to climb the stairs. I figured my mum would get annoyed looking after her type-A husband so I could spend a few nights there sharing the load. No doubt he'd want a bell to ring when he needed something and that would get old quickly.

As I pulled into the parking lot I saw an ambulance and could feel my heart in my chest, a thumping reminder this wasn't a social visit. But there were no sirens or paramedics rushing anywhere so whatever his injury, I assumed it was nothing serious.

My dad was a healthy guy—tall, lean, and an avid tennis player. Enjoying his retirement, renovating my childhood home was now keeping him busy. He'd recently finished a three-month master bathroom project he was very proud of. Friends had come over and he'd offered drinks in the bathroom so they could toast his craftsmanship. When I'd been home for dinner the week before, he flicked lights he'd installed under the kitchen cabinets and asked me to tell him how "bright" he was. As I drove away that night he'd stood at the front door, as he always did, waving at my tail lights.

I walked through the clubhouse and towards the bubble that housed the outdoor tennis courts in the winter months. I saw a good friend and tennis partner of my parents' coming towards me, his face blank and pale.

"It's over," he said.

"What's over?"

Our friend's face told me this injury was not a broken leg.

His eyes stared straight through me as I pushed the revolving doors into the bubble. It was quiet except for the fan whirring to keep the bubble inflated. A small crowd of people in athletic gear and paramedic uniforms surrounded my dad's body on the ground.

Despite all of his plans to grow old, my strong, witty, vivacious dad was dead.

Innocence shattered, I was no longer a carefree kid. My fresh breakup suddenly seemed like a skinned knee as I learned in an instant how painful life could be.

That Saint Patrick's Day, the first time I went out with friends since my dad passed away, I sat in the pub quietly. Soaked in grief, I was highly antisocial until a friend introduced me to a guy with sparkly green eyes wearing a horrible purple plaid shirt. He stunk of beer but was kind and funny. We got swept up in conversation and I found it refreshing to talk to someone unaware of my circumstance, and what I had lost.

The first few dates with Paul were long walks that ended in dinner, drinks and kisses. We stayed up late, talking about our families, our darkest secrets, and giggling hysterically. We went to concerts, took spontaneous weekends away, and drove around playing loud country music. We hosted dinner parties and snuggled to keep warm in long nightclub line-ups. We laughed a lot. I thought about how my dad would've liked him.

Paul was younger than me and my plan had always been to end up with someone older. He was Irish and I figured an Aussie or a Canadian would make a more suitable partner given my family background, so I didn't take the relationship too seriously. But then he moved in, and then we went travelling, and then he introduced me to his family. One weekend while snowshoeing in Whistler, he pulled champagne and fuzzy peaches out of his backpack, got down on one knee and asked me to marry him.

We bought an apartment and began planning a wedding. While on holiday in Peru, hiking Machu Picchu, I realized my period was late. Blaming my nausea on the altitude seemed easy in the moment but I bought a pregnancy test the evening we returned home. An hour later, we stood in our bathroom together, waiting for the lines to show up. The plan had been to have a wedding in Ireland and then to talk about a family, not the other way around.

At my twenty-week ultrasound, we found out there were issues with the baby's health. After several appointments and tests, a soft-spoken nurse told us the baby had congenital heart disease. The scans had shown a transposition of the great arteries, a congenital heart defect, as well as a ventricular septal defect, and an atrial septal defect. Our baby would need open-heart surgery. Through all of the diagnoses, uncertainty and testing, I wondered what my dad would have said. I imagined how his quest for problem-solving would play out as we prepared for an uncertain future. He would have done research and provided stats proving our baby would pull through. He would've found stories of Olympic athletes who had similar procedures and went on to excel. He would have stayed strong for us, armed with information when emotions were too much.

Paul and I got married in the living room of our apartment, just the two of us, a celebrant, and two friends who thought they were coming over for brunch. My husband insisted on wearing his Gaelic football jersey and matching socks. I wore a cotton maternity dress. It wasn't the white wedding we'd had in mind. My dad didn't get to give me away and there was no daddy-daughter dance.

The two most important men in my life would never meet.

A few weeks later, after twenty-four hours of labour, our son Declan was born by Caesarean. We gave him my dad's middle name, Craig. He was taken straight to the Pediatric Intensive Care Unit where he was immediately hooked up to oxygen, many monitors, and his tiny body was pricked all over for blood samples.

When I got a look at my son for the first time I didn't think he looked like mine. I didn't feel the rush of emotion and love I had anticipated. I was tired and wanted to go back to my room to rest and heal. I didn't want to be in the intensive care unit surrounded by strangers, constant beeping, green walls, and the smell of sanitizer. I was surprised by how little interest I had in my baby.

As testing continued, his condition became more complicated. There was muscle covering a valve that hadn't been seen on the scans. The surgeon didn't want to operate straight away after all. When we heard the hospital was sending us home after nine days with our baby still in heart failure, to be kept alive by an intense and complicated cocktail of medicine, I was petrified. We'd been told he wouldn't be coming home for weeks so we were completely unprepared.

At home, Paul emptied out a Tupperware tub filled with Christmas ornaments and washed it. We folded the blanket the nurses had given us and laid the baby down inside. He was so weak he barely even cried. He didn't look like either one of us. His chin was flat and his head was round. I didn't think he was cute, and said so often, which frustrated my husband. I knew I was afraid of getting attached to this new little person in our apartment, in case he wasn't a permanent member of our family.

Our baby rarely fussed but we had an around-the-clock feeding and medication schedule that left little time for sleep. I tried to breastfeed but he was too frail to suck for more than a few minutes so I pumped, sterilized bottles, and then boiled water for formula. My family was supportive but the absence of my dad was palpable.

After three weeks of the baby's weight steadily falling, the doctors put him on a feeding tube and a diet of disgusting-smelling formula available only by prescription. Nurses showed us how to maneuver the tube up through his nose down into his stomach as he screamed.

At six and a half months, our skinny boy, who had yet to sit, crawl, or roll went in for open-heart surgery. Early on a Tuesday, we dropped him off at Children's Hospital. We were told to hope for the best but to understand there may be complications. Kissing his cheeks goodbye and waving as an unfamiliar nurse carried him down the sterile hallway, it felt like a piece of my heart was walking away. Despite his weakness, he had learned to smile and looked back at us grinning obliviously as he disappeared into pre-op. The hospital gave us a pager and instructed us to be back in five hours, or if the pager beeped.

My husband and I went for brunch, at a place we'd been wanting to try but there was always a line. Despite incredible stress, we both knew this was a turning point. From here things would either get way worse or way better so we made a pact to enjoy our few hours together and try to be present, a reminder to one another that we would be okay. We window-shopped, laughed at overpriced furniture and talked about unimportant things, something we'd almost forgotten how to do since becoming parents. We were still in disbelief that we had such an ill child. Both healthy ourselves, it didn't make sense. We often wondered why we'd been chosen for this kind of challenge. I wondered the same about my dad and why he'd had his life cut short with so much of it left to live. It seemed cruel that my dad's healthy heart had stopped without warning while my son had been born broken, with a chance to repair his heart and live.

The pager never beeped so we returned to the hospital to learn the surgery had gone well but the baby's temperature wasn't regulating. It wasn't until hours later that the cardiology team was willing to call the operation a success. Dr G's nimble, brilliant hands had saved our son's life. Nine days later we took him home and at last, he began to thrive. His cheeks got pink, fat, and cuter, and our bond got stronger. We finally felt safe as a family of three.

I never knew grief before the day my dad died but I have known it several times since. I would give anything to see my father playing with my son, now a rambunctious five-year-old with a faint scar down his chest. He'd be so charmed by my daughter Fiona, the cuddly younger sister and animated storyteller. Knowing my kids will never meet my dad is debilitating at times. He would have wanted to know them; love them, teach them to skate, laugh at their jokes, play cards, build castles with them, and he didn't get the chance. And they'll never know all that they're missing.

These days, I make plans but never as optimistically or confidently as before. There's a piece missing and always will be. Things will be disrupted; I expect it.

Jenn is passionate about normalizing uncomfortable conversations and gets annoyed by mismanaged expectations. Just talk about it, people! She recently published a kids' book about anxiety called* Josie's Busy Calendar*, which could explain why she's so good at list-making. A long walk alone with a podcast is her go-to for relaxation. With two rambunctious kids to look after, Jenn can often be heard saying "I don't want us to be late."

@JENN_WINT

Burned Down

On December 12, 2015, at 2:30 a.m., the phone on my bedside table rang, waking me from an exhausted sleep. It was the landlord for my business.

"There's been a fire, come down now if you want to try to salvage anything."

Adrenaline flooded my body as I woke my husband, Alec. We threw on our clothes and raced over to find the bright red and white lights of three fire trucks piercing through the pitch-black night, the thick and overpowering smell of smoke, fire retardant foam blanketing the parking lot, and every window shattered by the intense heat. As I stood staring at the smouldering building a firefighter approached us. I saw his lips move but I couldn't hear his words. I opened my mouth to speak but there was no sound, only streams of tears falling. I placed my hands on my pregnant belly and felt the ground beneath me collapse.

I graduated from naturopathic medical school in 2013, completely inspired, but nervous to set up my own small business for the first time. Alec and I followed our intuition, took a huge leap and moved across the country to British Columbia. Although Squamish was the town that initially called us out west, we settled a bit further north in another small mountain village. With pennies to our name and a staggering amount of student debt, I began setting up my first humble practice. We struggled to start our lives in our new home. Alec worked an all-consuming job in hospitality while completing a master's degree in education, and we prioritized my business by putting off all our other financial goals.

After a year of struggling it became apparent we weren't getting ahead financially and we were in fact drowning in our student debt. Our bright future had contracted into darkness. When I reached out for help, the advice we received plunged me into the depths of shame and despair: Alec and I were told to file for bankruptcy. While I agreed we were out of options, I grappled with accepting the reality of bankruptcy which was equal to personal failure in my mind.

I reinvested every dollar I made back into my business and also worked a part-time job to keep the office afloat while I whittled our family budget down to the barest of necessities—always saying no to the extras, be it a glass of wine, a night out with friends, or a desperately needed new winter coat.

I appeared to be holding strong on the outside but I didn't let anyone know the crumbling that was happening on the inside as feelings of inadequacy, unworthiness, and scarcity dominated my every waking moment.

And then....when I thought it couldn't get any worse, my practice burned to the ground.

A group of under-aged kids set fire to the cardboard dumpster in the back alley, which burned out of control and spread to the building. Five-and-a-half months pregnant, broke, disillusioned, and devastated—I had lost it all.

Paralyzed about what to do next, the world was no longer safe and secure. I lost faith in the inner guidance that had led me down this path, and I questioned whether there was any good in the world.

And yet, as I watched in horror while the fire destroyed my business, a little flutter in my womb called my attention inwards—look here it told me, look here.

Tears streamed down my face and a softness entered my body. I vowed to focus on the beautiful being of light growing within me. My way forward was to nourish this tiny seed of hope, full of possibility. I knew that was all I needed to do.

And so, I poured every ounce of my attention into holding space for what was forming inside me and without knowing what it would mean, said yes to surrender and transformation. Years later I would realize the enormity of the threshold I had crossed that night.

After the fire I made radical changes. We had been living unhappily in Pemberton and two weeks after the fire we moved down to Squamish, the beautiful town that had originally called us to British Columbia. I prioritized my own healing. I planned to take a full year off with our baby instead of rushing to restart my naturopathic practice. I turned to a full-time job selling stretchy pants so I could continue to accumulate enough hours to earn a paid maternity leave, and struggled daily to show up to a job that wasn't fulfilling. Being reduced from a physician to an entry level stretchy-pant sales person consumed me with shame.

I felt like I was fumbling around in the dark, unsure and unsteady, and yet driven forward by an unknown force. I made sure to get up every day at the same time, I ate what my pregnant body craved, I walked in nature, I turned inwards, spending time connecting with the growing power in my pelvis, and I showed up to the stretchy-pant store. The numbing rhythm of folding stretchy pants, hundreds of pants a night, into perfectly symmetrical piles was something I could do. Slowly and surely as my hands were kept busy folding, new friendships were formed and I began to thaw.

Nestled by the warmth of a wood fire, I gave birth to Violet in our home with the support of Alec, our doula and two midwives. The experience was everything I wanted her birth to be and it was deeply healing—it proved I could trust my instincts and safely ride the waves of wild power when they came.

During the four months between the fire and Violet's birth I was able to collect the broken pieces of my ego, my shattered expectations, and my beliefs of what life was about. And in gluing myself back together I gathered the strength I needed to bring Violet into this world.

Caring for Violet came easily in the beginning and she taught me the power of simplicity, sleep, love, and devotion. We didn't have much, but we had everything she needed which in turn was exactly what I needed.

After those deeply healing first months in our newborn nest, I slowly, tenuously emerged back into the world. I was easily disoriented and overwhelmed. I had been opened up completely, stripped naked, and was as vulnerable as my newborn. Every time I contemplated my way forward on a professional level I panicked.

How the hell was I supposed to care for my beautiful daughter, provide financially for my family, reengage with my entrepreneurial spirit, all while feeling raw inside? All I wanted to do was retreat back into that blissful land of snuggles and the precious quiet mornings when I would hear the promise of a new day in the first birdsongs at dawn.

We made safe, responsible decisions in order to provide for our family while I put my dreams for restarting my naturopath business on hold. Alec finally began teaching and took on a second job at night while I stayed home with Violet that first year. When I returned to work, I joined a clinic as an associate and went back to school for two semesters so I could renew my nursing license and return to a better-paying part-time job.

Slowly, I started to become aware of the fear of scarcity that had completely taken over my world view. The professional devastation forced me to reevaluate deeply held beliefs about money, materialism, success, and my self-worth. Not only had I mistakenly internalized the financial collapse and arson fire as proof that I didn't belong in the land of entrepreneurship, I had also seen it as a personal failure. I began to realize how my determined desire to do it all on my own was actually suffocating me. Somewhere along the way I had become so scared that I stopped trusting my inner guidance—I had given my power away and in doing so had limited myself in every way possible.

Having Violet made me question everything: who am I, what do I value most in this world, what inspires me, what is sacred to me, what kind of mother do I want to be, what are the gifts

I have to offer, what is my legacy? As I focused on the simplicity of our daily rhythms, I also chose to focus on caring for myself with radical compassion and discipline. I returned in a more formal and devoted way to my longtime love, nature, as my biggest source of support and inspiration. I trusted the forests and streams as our daily muse for play, curiosity, and my continued healing.

Having Violet helped me rediscover my fullness and redefine my power.

Having Violet also forced me to abandon my stubborn independence and ask for help. And slowly, one by one, the most extraordinary women started appearing in our family's life at just the right time. We were no longer alone. We were surrounded by the most loving tribe of women—women who inspired me to continue mothering from my heart, women who cared for Violet while I worked and studied, a mother-daughter combo who welcomed Violet into their family and loved her as if she were their own, women who encouraged me open up my heart to Gaia and listen for her wisdom, women who walked with me and witnessed the tenderness of my soul, women who supported me through the birth of our second daughter Juniper, women who loaned me the finances I needed to restart my practice, and women who gently encouraged me out of my reluctant entrepreneurial shell and taught me how to turn my desires for work-life balance into a reality. Each one of these women filled my heart to overflowing with love and connection.

That fateful night of the fire when I was unable to speak up, Alec asked the firefighter to look for my degrees that had been hanging on the wall. That was all, just my degrees. His simple request was for me to walk away from the fire with a tangible reminder of the knowledge and skill that can never be taken away from me, that everything I need is already inside.

The fire brought Alec and I closer, bonded in the determination to get through life's challenges together. The fire created the opportunity to question the limiting beliefs and structures I had unknowingly adopted. The fire forced me to go within and find an unshakable strength, and encouraged me to dream again. The fire gave us the freedom to completely reimagine our lives and redefine what was worthy of our precious time and resources.

Rebuilding our lives proved that we are capable of creating something from seemingly nothing.

This journey has taught me the value and potency of the intangible: the power when I connect with my deepest wisdom and trust in my worth, the expansive softness in my heart as one of my babes melts into my chest, the contagious spark of joy and laughter, the magic when we are held in love and supported by another, the courage to open up and receive gifts from strangers, the passion in my soul as I practice my craft, and the wisdom I receive from the old-growth cedars through my sacred connection with nature. For the longest time I thought the fire was pure devastation, but now

I see that because of its flames my life is now full of the things that are most sacred and valuable to me.

♥

Lyndsey is a kitchen whiz with a knack for making healthy food delicious. Every day begins with morning meditation and green tea. On cold mornings, her pillow-sit includes a fuzzy sparkly unicorn onesie and blazing fire in the wood-burning fireplace. She is an introvert who is most comfortable frolicking in the forest or by a river. Lyndsey doesn't like cleaning, which is tough because a messy house gives her anxiety. She's a great listener who loves to hold spiritual space for others and was born to be a naturopathic doctor.

♥

Afterword

Wow, Volume 2!

Less than two years ago we had a dream to create a series of books to explore stories of motherhood that are often left untold. The funny, terrible, awkward, painful, joyful, stories that are rarely talked about, seldom passed down, and never shared, because the thought of being just a little (or a LOT) vulnerable is too goddamn scary.

We often forget how alike we are. Despite the fact that no two life journeys are ever the same, universal themes and our shared experiences connect us, and through this dialogue we begin to realize just how similar we really are.

These books are our *Field of Dreams*. The pages offer a protective space, where every woman who shows up feels held and capable of opening her heart to the possibilities this "conversation" carries.

Just like the movie, The MomBabes keep walking through the cornfields and into each other's lives. The sacred opportunity to write stories where we begin as mothers and finish as sisters is something we will never take for granted.

All good things start at home, and for this book we all ended here, too. At home with ourselves, with each other, truly accepting that we are worth the work, and our stories matter.

Our legacy matters.

So, here's the thing. We believe in the magic of story. We believe there is infinite value in the wisdom that is grown, inspired, and encouraged within our own community through the sharing of our experiences.

Thank you for reading, for being one of us, and for opening your heart.

Here's to Volume 3!

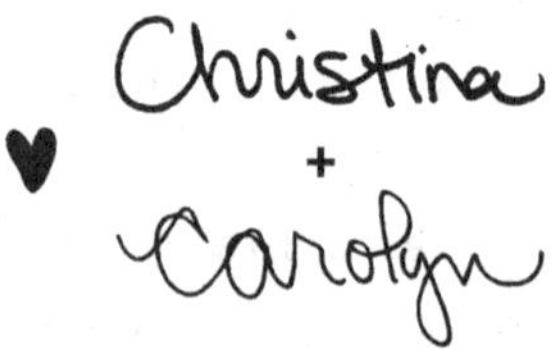

Acknowledgments

TO OUR LITTLE BABES: PIPER, REECE + QUINN
This legacy is for you! Remember, you can do and be anything. We love you more than you know.

TO OUR MOM: DORIS
Our forever cheerleader. If there is ever only one person in the stands, it'll be Doris.

TO OUR HUSBANDS: PETER AND BRADY
Thank you for always giving us the signal to swing away.

TO OUR TSPA DREAM TEAM: MEGAN, TARA, IRA & KRISTY:
Thank you for leaping with us again. For your endless support, encouragement, and virtual high-fives. Let's keep hitting home runs together!

AND TO OUR AUTHORS:
Thank you for believing in us, thank you for believing in you. Keep writing your stories. We love you.

CHRISTINA WALSH AND CAROLYN TURKINGTON

We're The MomBabes. We're sisters and we can be yours too.

Christina is a mom to two little girls and Carolyn has a little boy. We live in the suburbs outside of Vancouver and only Carolyn drives a minivan.

We are here to flip the script and show moms that no matter how monumental these years can be in transforming who you are, we know your dreams are still in there. **The MomBabes books are permission slips to all moms**—an invitation to rediscover your dreams, dust them off, edit them, wrap them up in a beautiful cover, and move them to the front of the bookshelf.

themombabes.com

@themombabes

photo credit: Grinning Weasel Photography